THE WINDJAMMERS

The Seafarers THE WINDJAMMERS

The Cover: While crewmen aloft furl
the mizzen royal, the British bark
Garthpool knifes her way through sunlit
seas as she approaches Queenstown,
Ireland, with grain in 1926. Back in
home waters after a 121-day passage from
Australia, she towers majestically above
a passing tramp steamer in this rendering
by British artist Derek G. H. Gardner.

The Title Page: Bound in brass and
studded with brass stars, this mahogany
wheel, five feet in diameter, was the
helm of the bark *Kaiulani.* The last
American square-rigger, she eventually
became a mastless log barge in the
Philippines, ferrying exotic woods from
forest to sawmill, after 43 years under sail.

The Seafarers

THE WINDJAMMERS

by Oliver E. Allen

AND THE EDITORS OF TIME-LIFE BOOKS

TIME-LIFE BOOKS, AMSTERDAM

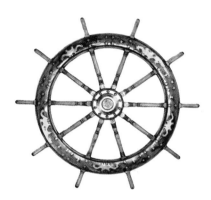

The Seafarers
Editorial Staff for *The Windjammers*:
Editor: George G. Daniels
Picture Editor: John Conrad Weiser
Designer: Herbert H. Quarmby
Text Editors: Anne Horan, Sterling Seagrave
Staff Writers: William C. Banks, Carol Dana,
Stuart Gannes, Gus Hedberg
Chief Researchers: Martha T. Goolrick,
Charlotte A. Quinn
Researchers: Mary G. Burns, Patti H. Cass, Philip Brandt
George, W. Mark Hamilton, Barbara Levitt,
Elizabeth L. Parker
Art Assistant: Michelle René Clay
Editorial Assistant: Adrienne George

Correspondents: Elisabeth Kraemer (Bonn); Margot
Hapgood, Dorothy Bacon (London); Susan Jonas, Lucy T.
Voulgaris (New York); Maria Vincenza Aloisi,
Josephine du Brusle (Paris); Ann Natanson (Rome).
Valuable assistance was also provided by: Wibo
Vandelinde, Janny Hovinga (Amsterdam); Leny Heinen
(Bonn); Lance Keyworth (Helsinki); Penny Newman,
Judy Aspinall (London); John Dunn (Melbourne);
Carolyn T. Chubet, Miriam Hsia (New York); John Scott
(Ottawa); Al Prince (Papeete); Janet Zich (San Francisco);
Mario Planet (Santiago); Mary Johnson (Stockholm);
Bill Carroll (Toronto).

The editors are indebted to Champ Clark, Barbara Hicks
and Richard M. Seamon for their help in the preparation
of this book.

The Author:
Oliver E. Allen, the great-great grandson
of a tea-clipper merchant whose square-
riggers sailed from Philadelphia to Canton
in the 1840s, is a full-time writer living in
Pelham, New York. A former Planning Director of Time-Life Books, he has written
on a wide range of subjects, from national
politics to gardening.

The Consultants:
John Horace Parry, Professor of Oceanic
History at Harvard University, was educated at Cambridge University, where he took
his Ph.D. He served in the Royal Navy during World War II, rising to the rank of commander. He is the author of 10 books, including *The Discovery of the Sea, The
Spanish Seaborne Empire, Europe and a
Wider World* and *Trade and Dominion.*

Giles M. S. Tod, a lifelong expert on sailing
vessels, is the author of *Last Sail Down East*
and numerous other writings about ships
and the sea. In 1934 he observed windjammers firsthand when he served as a crewman on the four-masted Finnish bark *Herzogin Cecilie* on a passage from England to
Australia and back around Cape Horn.

Dr. Jürgen Meyer, author of four books on
the history of German seafaring, is the curator of the Shipping Department at the Altonaer Museum, in Hamburg, Germany.

Contents

The glorious age of tall ships

Windjammer—the word rang like an insult. And that was the intention of hooting steamship crews, who used it to describe the huge square-rigged sailing vessels that were valiantly challenging the coming of steam on world trade routes. These monsters, they said, were far too gross and clumsy to sail neatly into the wind but had to be jammed into it, their yards braced way around on the backstays.

But the jibe became an accolade. For in truth, in their 50 years of useful life, the windjammers expressed the consummate majesty of sail and the climax of centuries of glorious evolution.

Scudding before a howling Cape Horn gale or running smartly before the trade winds, these white-winged tall ships were unparalleled in size, power and beauty. Many were twice as long as the graceful wooden clipper ships that had preceded them, and almost as swift. With acres of sail on their towering masts, they carried thousands of tons of nitrates, guano, coal, grain and timber around the world in their vast hulls.

From the outset, as they fought their way around Cape Horn and charged through the Southern oceans, the windjammers captured the hearts of sailors and landsmen alike. The *Potosi*, the *Preussen*, the *Herzogin Cecilie* and scores of others with wonderful names set and broke and reset records from Chile or Australia to Europe, surviving incredible storms and hardship. Even in their twilight, during the 1920s and 1930s, their driving spirit was to outsail all rivals. When the *Hougomont* raced the *Archibald Russell* from Australia to Ireland in 1927, her crew went so far as to scour her bottom while under way by dragging a wire under it—and won by four days. On the *Viking* in 1934 a man remarked that the barometer was up, presaging good weather. "To hell with a high glass!" snapped the captain. "We want it pointing to storm and getting us home."

That was the way of the windjammers. Steamships could ask for mild seas and bland skies, but windjammers thrived on brisk gales and fast passages, as befitted the final celebration of the glorious age of sail.

Furling the sails quickly in the face of a rising storm, Cape Horners crewing the four-masted bark Parma in the early 1930s pass gaskets around her ice-stiffened mainsail while balancing on footropes. When possible, they would observe the tradition of one hand for the ship, one hand for the sailor, but the stiffness of the great mainsail required the use of both hands, and only the force of the wind held the sailors firmly against the main yard.

Battered by a Pacific gale on the salmon run to Alaska in the early 1900s, crewmen of the Star of Finland drop a staysail and prepare to stow it, leaving only the storm sails aloft. A ship's boat at left has been torn loose from its cradle and lashings by the sea's fury. American windjammers in the salmon trade carried these boats, called gill-netters, on deck to tend salmon nets off the coast of Alaska. Once caught, the fish were cleaned and canned by Chinese workers, and then shipped to market.

Taking advantage of fine weather while bound from New York to Yokohama in August 1900, crewmen of the American four-masted bark Arthur Sewall haul a heavy sail to bend on a yard. Two other large square sails lie on the deck waiting to be bent to yards. At far left is the capstan used to heave the sails aloft. In heavy weather, windjammers often blew out their sails, so several suits were carried by ships that could afford them. Even then, sailors were constantly mending to lengthen the life of canvas.

Straining at the capstan bars, crewmen on the three-masted, full-rigged ship *Grace Harwar* in 1929 heave the main-topsail aloft as a westerly gale off Cape Horn subsides. When storms ended, more sail was cranked on to maintain top speed. Built in 1889, the *Grace Harwar* had already reached the ripe old age of 40 when she made this run from Australia to England with a load of grain. Yet old as she was, the *Grace Harwar* was able to hold her own in the annual grain races from Australia to Europe.

The weathered crewmen of a French windjammer soak up the sunshine as they mend sails on deck. Moments like these were the best times of the voyage, filled with jests and tall stories. French windjammers were called bounty ships because the government—with the intention of expanding trade —underwrote the costs of building and operating them. This subsidy made it possible for the shipowners of France to construct 212 new sailing vessels between the years 1892 and 1902.

Chapter 1

Gigantic descendants of the lovely clippers

Leaving New York behind, the windjammer Wavertree sets her shoulder to the sea in this re-creation of an 1895 scene by marine artist John Stobart.

t midnight she was first spotted as a distant shape on the moonlit horizon. By dawn her dimensions had grown to majestic size. Passengers and crew of the British liner crowded the rail to stare at the tall ship they were overtaking. She seemed an apparition from another age. A graceful, white-hulled bark, her four masts crowded with wind-taut sails, she belonged on an earlier ocean, on sea-lanes as yet unsullied by the smoke and soot of steamers.

The captain of the liner rang his engine-room telegraph and signaled for more power. He would give his passengers something to remember; he would close in swiftly on this old windjammer, dramatically cross her bows and then proceed on course for Rio de Janeiro. But on board the big steel bark in the South Atlantic that October morning in 1934, Captain Sven Eriksson had other ideas. To him, the *Herzogin Cecilie*, the 32-year-old ship under his command, was no weather-beaten anachronism; outbound from Belfast, Ireland, for Port Lincoln, South Australia, to take on a load of grain, she was to her master a useful deepwater cargo carrier, still capable of turning a profit while she did her share of the world's work. And no awkward liner with smoke-belching funnels and racketing engines was going to show Eriksson her stern—not with a fresh, fair wind piping up and the *Herzogin Cecilie* moving steadily toward her top speed.

The *Herzogin Cecilie* was German built but she had been under Finnish registry since the end of World War I. She was manned by seamen from many nations, with a core of mariners from Åland Island, midway between Finland and Sweden—tough young men in their teens and early 20s, bred to the sea and the hard-muscled life on hard-driven ships. Eriksson ordered his crew aloft to shake out more sail.

As the steamer drew closer, the *Herzogin Cecilie*'s royals, topmost sails of all, were sheeted home; the mighty windjammer was now wearing her full suit of 35 sails, an incredible 45,000 square feet of heavy canvas. Furious work on powerful deck-mounted winches braced the yards so that this vast expanse of sail picked up maximum drive from the rapidly freshening wind. Now it was blowing at 35 to 40 knots, close to gale force. The *Herzogin Cecilie*'s bow wave arced in the sunlight as she moved faster and faster—16 knots, then 17, almost 18. Her lee rail was awash. Green seas hissed past her quarter. It took two crewmen straining at her massive wheel to hold her on course.

For several moments, steamer and sailer ran side by side. Then slowly, steadily, the great sailing ship picked up speed on the steamer. And then she began to move away. As the liner slid inexorably astern, her captain blew three long blasts on his steam whistle in a graceful acknowledgment of defeat; he then dipped his red British ensign in salute to the victor. Aboard the *Herzogin Cecilie* Captain Eriksson dipped his blue and white Finnish colors in return.

The two ships bore off on divergent courses. Soon the *Herzogin Cecilie*'s masts dropped below the horizon. Her brief, proud triumph was over. Nor was it likely to be repeated. The last great age of sail, the magnificent era of the windjammers, was already drifting in the doldrums from which it would never escape. In truth, before that race across a windy reach of the Atlantic even started, the *Herzogin Cecilie* and all her sister ships were already doomed. But those who sailed the tall ships, and those who watched them pass—like all the passengers and crew of the liner on that sun-splashed October morning—knew quite well what Britain's Poet Laureate John Masefield had in mind when he wrote of the windjammers: "They mark our passage as a race of men,/ Earth will not see such ships as those again."

It is a sad irony of maritime history that merchant sailing ships like the *Herzogin Cecilie* reached their pinnacle of grace and power just at a time when steam-driven passenger liners and cargo carriers were coming to rule the sea-lanes of the world. The day of the windjammer was all too brief—only 60 years or so spanning the end of the 19th Century and the first third of the 20th. By then the lovely clipper ships of the mid-19th Century were already gone, their swift beauty no longer practical. In their day the clippers had logged fantastically quick passages to and from the Orient in their headlong races for a share of the tea trade. And they had carried vast armies of impatient fortune seekers westward around Cape Horn to the gold fields of California and Australia. But in 1869 the two American coasts were linked by rail. In that same year the

The ditch that doomed the days of sail

Sails fill the Suez Canal in this handsome but overly optimistic view before the channel was finished.

In the early 1860s the Suez Canal Company commissioned German artist Albert Rieger to paint a panorama of the waterway it was just then digging between the Mediterranean and the Red Sea. Working from maps and plans, Rieger painted an oil *(left)* that proved remarkably accurate when the canal went into service in 1869—save for one important detail. He depicted sailing ships in the canal, when in fact it was all but useless to seagoing sail. Though the canal was ideal for steamers, sailing was usually impossible in the narrow, often windless channel.

The omens were clear even before the canal was officially opened. Just hours before the inaugural ceremonies, a three-masted frigate became so desperately grounded in mid-channel that authorities threatened to blow her up if she could not be worked free. A year later the effect of the canal on the white-winged ships led builder Ferdinand de Lesseps to write sadly, "I apologize to the sailing vessels."

Suez Canal proved a godsend to steamships—and an exercise in futility for blue-water sailing vessels *(page 19)*. On some routes the new steamships began to cut weeks from the clippers' fastest voyages. Restricted in size and capacity by the requirements of their wooden construction, dependent upon the unpredictable weather instead of internal propulsion, the clippers simply became uneconomical.

After the clippers quit deepwater trade, most shipowners began to use steam power. Still, there were many diehards who remained absolutely convinced that the right sort of sailing ships could continue to compete. In the waning years of the 19th Century, the shipyards of Europe turned out a magnificent fleet of such sailing ships, which came to be known as the windjammers.

Lineal descendants of the clippers, the windjammers were built of iron and steel rather than wood. And the new ships were awesome in every dimension. Most were at least 300 feet long (the *Herzogin Cecilie* was 334; the average clipper 150) and some reached beyond 400 feet. Their masts, three feet thick at the base, towered as high as 200 feet above the keel; some of the yards from which the sails were suspended were more than 100 feet long and up to two feet in diameter at the center. The largest of their sails weighed a ton dry and far more when wet. Laid

Idle square-riggers jam a harbor jetty in Newcastle, Australia, in 1900 as they wait for cargoes of coal to ship to Chile and Peru. "The ships," said an apprentice on an English coal ship, "gave the impression of a forest of masts and spars and rigging, in a confused tangle against the skyline."

end to end, the wire and chain and manila line in their rigging would have stretched for miles.

This gigantic new breed of sailing ship could carry immense amounts of cargo—up to 8,000 tons—at impressive speeds over long distances on routes where the trade winds blew strongly and reliably. Under the command of skippers like Sven Eriksson, men who were experts in the intricate science of sail, they could hold their own with any other ship afloat. Indeed, Eriksson's victory over the liner was not particularly unusual: in some ways, on some routes, for some years, the windjammers proved to be better than steam.

What they could do superlatively well was carry the bulk raw materials from out-of-the-way places demanded by the very Industrial-Mechanical Age that in the end would spell their death. At the turn of the century, Europe's burgeoning factories needed more and more copper ore from Chile. The Continent's farmers were hard put to feed the ever-expanding cities without having fertilizer for their crops; Peru had this in abundance, in the bird droppings—called guano—that blanketed islands off the rocky coast, and Chile had fertilizer in the nitrate-rich soil of the Andean foothills. Lumber from the forests of the American Northwest was in great demand. So were coal from Australia and grain from that island-continent's vast interior.

But Chile, Peru, Australia and the American Northwest lay thousands of miles from Europe across some of the meanest waters on earth. Outbound vessels traveling westward had to contend with the gale-force winds that raged almost perpetually through the 10° of latitude known as the roaring forties. And off Cape Horn itself the winds lashed ships with sleet, snow and hail that swooped down from the slopes of the southern Andes. Squalls and fog hid the jagged rocks of the island tips of Tierra del Fuego and the hull-ripping fingers of icebergs broken off from the frozen wastes of Antarctica.

The windjammers enjoyed many advantages in those early days of steam. For one thing, they could survive in almost any sea and battle through frightful waves that would crumple smokestacks, douse steam boilers and shear off propellers like so much tin foil. In fair weather the steamers of the 1880s and 1890s could average seven knots. Windjammers could do better in all but the lightest or most adverse winds. The wind, moreover, was free. Coaling stations were few in the southern oceans, and what stations there were charged high prices. Vital fuel, burned in prodigious amounts, became more and more expensive as the steamers traveled farther from home. Fresh water for a steamer's boilers was also a constant problem, particularly on the parched coast of South America.

Even under optimum conditions, steamers were fearfully costly at sea and had to be kept on the go almost constantly if their owners were to make a profit. But the operating cost of a windjammer was economy itself. The great sailing vessel could even lie in a distant roadstead for weeks or months while she awaited a cargo, then load and sail home, still making a profit.

Around the turn of the century, while steamers were yet searching for their sea legs, there were thousands of windjammers plying the oceans in deepwater trade, and hundreds of firms competed for their share of the shipping business. Individually and in total, these magnificent vessels were the very zenith of sail, "the outcome," as maritime historian W. L. A. Derby wrote, "of centuries of experiment in the harnessing of wind-power to propulsive uses. Lacking the daintiness, the handiness and the sweet lines of their progenitors, they nevertheless represented, at their prime, sail's epitome of combined strength, seaworthiness, economy and longevity."

Steel was the great secret in the construction of windjammers. Steel bulkheads, hull plates, even masts made possible their strength and their size. Wood was virtually eliminated, used only for decks and for decorative trim, as in the master's saloon. And as size and strength increased by quantum jumps, major changes were effected in hull design. Gone were the rounded sides and bottoms of earlier wooden vessels; hulls were now built with straight sides and deep, flat bottoms that afforded fullest cargo capacity.

As ships grew larger and larger, three masts gave way to four, even to five. And sail plans began to change as well. The first windjammers built in the 1880s and 1890s were true full-rigged ships, with square sails on all their masts. But as masts were added new rigs were developed. A four-masted vessel, square-rigged on the fore-, main- and mizzenmasts but carrying on her fourth mast fore-and-aft sails, mounted parallel to the keel, proved to be more maneuverable than a full-rigged ship, and almost as fast. These barks, as they were called, became virtually the standard windjammer design, and for another reason besides maneuverability: their more manageable sails did not require so big a crew. Over the years, in fact, windjammers were sailed by increasingly smaller crews. A 1,500-ton clipper had usually been sailed by a crew of 50 to 60 men, but the crew of a 2,500-ton windjammer averaged less than 30 men. In the early 1930s the full-rigger *Grace Harwar* made a successful passage around the Horn with a crew of just 19.

As the size of hulls and the number of masts changed dramatically from the clipper days, so did the size of sails. With smaller crews, fewer men were available to go aloft to furl or unfurl sail—an arduous assignment even with plenty of hands on watch—so it made sense to limit the size of some of the canvas. Longer yards meant wider sails, but some of them were not so big now from top to bottom. Where the clipper had a single topgallant, the windjammer divided that sail in two to make an upper topgallant and a lower one *(pages 30-31)*. At the same time, some of the clipper's extra canvas was discarded—like the studding sails, which had hung out to port and starboard on booms that extended from the lower yards. It was too much work to set them, said windjammer sailors, and they were not worth the small increment in speed that they might provide. The clipper under full canvas, her studding sails set, had an almost triangular silhouette when she was viewed from ahead or astern. The windjammer reached higher and appeared more like a narrow rectangle.

Other advances on deck, long overdue, provided greater protection for the crew against the massive seas that could sweep across the decks in a

Using special thimbles held in their palms in order to force needles through the tough canvas, two sailmakers add boltropes to the edges of a windjammer sail while a third selects the sail's clew irons and earings, hanging sausage-like from the wall. Some 14,000 yards of canvas, miles of seams and thousands of stitches went into a windjammer suit.

storm and wash a man overboard with brutal ease. In the heyday of the windjammer there was no agency responsible for recording the number of men washed overboard or otherwise lost to the mountainous seas. But there were dozens every year. In addition to endangering the crew, green water on deck threatened the very existence of the ship because its crushing weight—estimated at 600 to 700 tons if the deck was deeply awash—lowered the hull significantly and affected its balance and seaworthiness.

A major innovation was the addition of a midship "island" that was larger than a clipper's deckhouse. A massive raised section across the waist of the ship, this island broke up the main deck into two smaller wells and dispersed rampaging seas. In many ships the island contained living quarters for both officers and crew, a much more convenient arrangement than having captain and mates aft and crew all the way forward in the forecastle. But old habits died hard at sea, and the crew's quarters were nevertheless still referred to as the fo'c's'le.

The island was connected to the poop deck aft and the fo'c's'le forward by raised catwalks, known as flying bridges, that helped the crew avoid deck water some of the time. German shipmasters went a step further in looking after their crews by rigging life nets along the sides of the deck wells whenever they entered stormy regions.

Windjammer helmsmen were also given added protection. A sailing-ship's wheel was traditionally located far aft, almost directly above the rudder, and helmsmen were terribly vulnerable to any following sea that broke over the stern, "pooping" the ship, as sailors called it. On the windjammer *Gogoburn* in 1899, a pooper smashed the wheel and threw the two helmsmen forward up against the base of the mizzenmast, where they were found bleeding and unconscious. The same rogue wave pitched the captain and a seaman overboard; both were lost.

Helmsmen were often lashed to the deck to prevent them from being washed over the side; even so, working the wheel in rough weather was an exhausting and perilous job. In some windjammers a protective cowling was installed just abaft the wheel. In others, particularly the big German barks, the wheel itself was eventually moved forward and positioned in the midship island, where it was safe from all but the most mammoth waves.

Perhaps the most significant change over other sailing ships was in the windjammer's rigging. With steel masts and steel yards came wire cable rope and chain rigging. It was heavy—the weight of masts, yards and rigging on a four-masted bark exceeded 60 tons—but it was infinitely stronger than the old wood and manila-rope rigging. As a rule, only the ends of the running rigging—lines that were used by the crew to control the yards and sails—were still made of manila rope. The introduction of winches eased the backbreaking work of hoisting and lowering the heaviest sails and yards, those on the bottom segments of the masts; now only the upper sails and yards had to be worked by hand. Winches also simplified bracing—changing the angle of the larger yards to take better advantage of the wind. The brace winches were the creation of an innovative Scottish shipmaster named Captain J. C. B. Jarvis, who in the 1870s and 1880s challenged many of sail's traditional methods. A set of hefty, hand-wound conical drums, the Jarvis winches were used to loosen the brace lines leading to one side of the yardarms at the same time that those on the other side were being tightened. A job that previously had required a dozen men could now be accomplished by two or three. Alas, as is so often the case, Jarvis' genius was honored more abroad than at home. Jarvis winches were not installed on many British ships. But other nations knew a good thing when they saw it and soon made the winches standard equipment.

Steel rigging made for some unusual sounds. As windjammer authority W. L. A. Derby put it, "The tautness and power of a steel and wire top-hamper will combine, in bad weather, to produce a diapason such as can nowhere be heard except aboard a big, heavy-laden sailer. She becomes, as it were, a giant organ played by the heavy hands of wind and sea. Powerful gusts pluck at the tensed shrouds and straining backstays like fingers at harp-strings. Where some stays give forth a deep booming note, others hum wildly, like telegraph wires, under the stress. Halliards twang like banjo-gut, and a continuous and plaintive moaning comes from the rigging-screws. The gale roars through the slacker running-rigging, whose heavy blocks beat a mad tattoo against the steel spars. As she rolls, scuppers under, the steel wash-ports clang to and fro, and all the while the great seas break alongside or crash aboard to swirl from poop to fo'c'sle, battering at the deck-house doors and striving to wrench off the hatch tarpaulins. Every strake and frame of the labouring hull groans with her travail; while the thunder of wet storm canvas, and the staccato patter of squalls of driven hail add to that almost indescribable cacophony, the song of driven sail."

The fantastic strength of these stout steel ships never ceased to amaze—and not simply at sea, as they battled through the worst that the elements had to offer. One of the most graphic illustrations of their might and power occurred in the port of Philadelphia, on a fine summer's day in 1893, in full view of a crowd of awe-struck landlubbers.

The windjammer was a four-masted British bark named the *Wanderer*, and somehow she managed to break loose from one of her two tugs during the docking maneuvers. With the second tug struggling helplessly alongside, she began drifting downstream toward a wharf, Pier 22. John Masefield, who wrote a history of the vessel and celebrated her in one of his finest poems, described what happened next: "This pier was piled with empty casks. The *Wanderer* drove the tug into the pier, and scattered the pile of casks in all directions: the tug's crew jumped ashore as she struck. The *Wanderer* dragged past Pier 22, went on into Pier 23, struck it, and went past it towards the Vine Street Dock, where the ferry boat, *Cooper's Point*, was taking passengers for Camden. Some men in the police tug, *Stockley*, then lying near the wharf, shouted to the passengers to jump clear. The passengers scrambled for the shore, but before many had landed the *Wanderer*'s bows went into the *Cooper's Point*, cut through the strong plank fenders at her port side, holed her, smashed up her superstructure, cleared her upper deck, and 'squeezed her funnel out.' Some people and horses were knocked down; two ladies and a man were slightly hurt."

The collision finally checked the bark's drift, and her rudder was slightly damaged as she came to rest. The cost of repairing the *Cooper's Point* came to $7,000. As for the *Wanderer*, she fixed her rudder in short order, loaded case oil and sailed for Calcutta.

No wooden-hulled little clipper ship could have caused such havoc, or survived the battering with so little damage to herself. And certainly no wooden-hulled ship of whatever size could have carried some of the cargoes that became the windjammers' stock in trade. Chilean nitrates, for example, were highly flammable; if a cargo caught fire, only a steel-hulled ship had any hope of survival, and even then the blaze had to be extinguished quickly or the ship would be gutted.

Coal, which the windjammers also carried in great quantities, had its own peculiar problems. If it became damp while in an enclosed hold, it might begin smouldering from spontaneous combustion. The hidden fire could burn for days before being detected; it was then extremely difficult to douse. In many cases there was no choice but to try containing the fire by sealing the hold, meanwhile heading for port as decks and hull became hotter and hotter. A celebrated fire aboard the four-masted

Scrambling up the mizzenmast rigging, crewmen of the four-masted steel bark Queen Margaret hurry aloft to help furl unwanted sail on a passage from New York to Australia in 1905. On such a vessel the incredibly complex system of rigging needed to support the masts and control the sails could require more than 16 miles of cordage, wire and chain.

bark *Cedarbank*, hauling coal from Newcastle, Australia, to San Francisco in 1893, burned for more than a month. The pumps were kept going night and day; on several occasions, explosions blew off hatch covers, but the crew battened them down again. Acrid blue smoke made all work difficult, and the pitch melted in the seams of the deck. Still the floating furnace sailed on. Not until she made port was the fire put out. A wooden ship would never have made port at all.

Windjammers were sometimes compared to floating storage bins, virtual warehouses on the move. No one expected them to be as fleet-footed as the earlier clippers, and indeed they were not. But they nevertheless kept astonishing everyone—except possibly their captains and crews—with the swiftness of their passages. The records for one-day runs by sailing ships are all held by the clippers: the American *Champion of the Seas* once racked up 465 miles from noon to noon, for an average of better than 19 knots, and the *Flying Scud* claimed 449 miles, for an average of 18. By comparison, the best record set by a windjammer was 378 miles, an average of less than 16 knots, made by the German five-masted bark *Potosi* in 1900. Still, in comparable port-to-port passages over the long haul, the best windjammer achievements are nothing to be ashamed of. The record on the London-to-Melbourne route—60 days—was held by the British wool clipper *Thermopylae*; in 1934, the German barks *Padua* and *Priwall*, far more heavily loaded, both managed to traverse a longer route from Hamburg to Port Lincoln, Australia, in 65 days.

The records come closest in absolute top speeds. Once again the clippers did better, but the windjammers came close. The highest speed ever achieved under commercial sail was by an American clipper, the *James Baines*, which reached 21 knots in 1856. Seventy-five years later, on June 2, 1931, the *Herzogin Cecilie*—the windjammer that outsailed the ocean liner—reached a speed of $20\frac{3}{4}$ knots off the northeast coast of Denmark. The circumstances were admittedly freakish.

The *Herzogin Cecilie* happened to be sailing from Wales to Finland through the Kattegat, the sound that separates Denmark from Sweden. In the relative shelter of these waters, there were no long reaches in which great waves could build up. Thus, in a strong wind, a ship could attain her best speed. And that is what happened to the *Herzogin Cecilie*. In the late afternoon the wind quickened to gale force. Suddenly, with the tide in her favor, she was flying.

As the ship heeled over at more than 30°, an observer on board computed her speed between two lightships during a 75-minute period, and his figures showed she was moving at 34 feet per second, or almost 21 knots. Darkness was approaching and there was some question of stopping the run since Copenhagen Sound just ahead was narrow and congested. But the bark's rush through the seas was so spectacular that Sven Eriksson, her captain, decided to sail on.

All night long she raced southward. Eriksson repeatedly sent up blue flares to warn other craft of her approach. "Not a soul on board turned in," the *Herzogin Cecilie*'s historian wrote later. "Normal watches were abandoned and all hands stood by, unable to do other than watch the great white bark tear madly southward, wondering, no doubt, whether her canvas would withstand the strain of such driving. She fled through the Sound, past Hven Island, overtaking steamers bound in the same direction as though they were anchored."

At last, as she passed Copenhagen at dawn, the gradually diminishing wind fell to a gentle breeze, and she continued her voyage in more leisurely fashion. Yet her earlier burst of speed had been enough to carry her 164 miles in 13 hours, for an average of almost 13 knots.

What made her feat all the more amazing was the fact that she was due for a dry docking to have her bottom cleaned as she was foul below the water line. Windjammer men have long speculated how fast she might have gone had she been fresh from an overhaul.

Only a superbly skilled captain and crew in a well-rigged ship could produce high speeds in a windjammer. The working of such a vessel was an art in itself; as one veteran sailor remarked, "one bungling fool and one stranded wire, one too-chafed piece of service could ruin the manoeuvre."

The rigging of these ultimate sailing ships was a triumph of intricate logic—a logic based on centuries of practical experience. The spires of masts and spider webs of lines reaching to the sky were actually two separate systems that were virtually independent of each other. The standing rigging, the shrouds and stays whose function was to fix the masts firmly in place, consisted of wire cables. The shrouds were rigged in pairs with cross wires known as ratlines, which made rope ladders for the crew to climb aloft.

Climbing all the way to the topmost foreroyal yard would take an experienced hand no more than two or three minutes. An apprentice seaman might take as long as half an hour—much of which would be spent conquering his terror at the dizzying height as he inched higher and higher. The backstays, heavy wires that led aft from the masts down to fastenings along the sides of the ship, were sometimes used by show-off veterans for a quick sliding descent to the deck, although they sometimes ended up with hands coated with tar or cut by frayed wire. More prudent sailors clambered down as they went up: using the ratlines. At sea they always went up or down the windward side so that the force of the wind would blow them onto the rigging rather than away from it. Going aloft in a storm, wrote one sailor, "called for all a man's strength, because the wind literally flattened him against the shrouds and he had to fight for every step upwards or downwards."

The running rigging that made up the second system controlled the sails and the yards. In the days before winches, hauling on halyards, which moved yards up or down when sails were furled or unfurled, was heavy work, often accompanied by chanteys or at least by shouting or loud grunting ("Hey-ya, hey-ho!" or "Pulley-haul!"). When a sail was furled, it was first gathered in to its yard by lines that reached to the deck. Then the crew would scramble aloft to make it fast.

Tough as deck work was, things could be worse aloft—especially when the weather turned sour. Then sails had to be doused quickly lest an overcanvased ship sail itself right under the waves. Once a sail was hauled up to its yard, the seamen would go aloft to the yard, then out along it, their feet on the footrope suspended beneath, their hands on the

The Plimsoll line: sign of safety

In frock coat and top hat, a monstrous camera in tow, Samuel Plimsoll was a curious sight in England's port towns at the start of the windjammer era in the early 1870s. More curious still was the errand that led a member of Parliament to mix with sailors, most of whom had no property and therefore no vote.

With a fervor verging on fanaticism, Plimsoll in 1870 had taken up a crusade against what he called "coffin ships"—unsafe cargo vessels, sail and steam alike, that each year killed hundreds of sailors. Facing strong opposition in Parliament, Plimsoll set out to document the worst abuses and to enlist public support. The result, in 1873, was *Our Seamen,* a book that used shocking case studies and government statistics to demonstrate that overloading and unseaworthiness were primary causes of England's shipwrecks. Plimsoll also included piteous tales—a sailor's widow tearfully eking out a living sewing by the light of a garret window—even photos of pallid, grim-lipped women surrounded by their black-garbed fatherless broods.

The volume—which laid the blame at the feet of money-grubbing shipowners and an indifferent government—had the desired effect. By 1875 a bill was before the House of Commons containing one of Plimsoll's pet reforms—a mandatory line painted on the side of cargo ships to indicate the maximum safe loading depth. But on July 22 Prime Minister Disraeli unexpectedly moved to withdraw the measure, probably under pressure from shippers who claimed that the restrictions would give an advantage to foreign rivals.

Jumping to his feet, Plimsoll charged shipowners in the House with "murderous tendencies" in delaying the bill. As Plimsoll stormed from the chamber, his wife, seated in the ladies' gallery, let summaries of Plimsoll's protest flutter into the press gallery below.

Plimsoll's outburst made headlines and ultimately forced Parliament to pass the Unseaworthy Ships Bill. But the law left placement of the load line up to shipowners, some of whom jokingly painted the stripe on their ships' decks. In 1890, however, Parliament authorized the Board of Trade to fix the mark of the "Plimsoll line," and by the 1930s most nations had adopted it.

Samuel Plimsoll, as portrayed by Vanity Fair in 1873.

The official load line is a 12-inch circle bisected by an 18-inch line. To account for varying water densities and seasonal conditions, a separate insignia shows loading heights for fresh water (F) and Winter North Atlantic water (WNA).

jackstay—the rail along the top of the yard. The men would pull and punch at the canvas to spill the remaining air out of it.

Author and seafarer Alan Villiers described the technique from personal experience: "You begin the fight at the center of the yard, thumping down the canvas that is bellying back, hauling up the canvas that is hanging down beneath the yard and against the foot-ropes, until you have all the canvas up on the yard beneath your stomach; then you make a skin of the last foot or so closest to the yard, punch all the rest neatly into that, brace your knees against the yard and roll her up, whip the gasket around, and the job's done!"

All sailors were well acquainted with the rule, "One hand for the ship and one for yourself." Still, accidents happened all too frequently, and sailors took them for granted. "It was not that they were careless," explained one veteran seaman. "It just did not occur to them that their work was dangerous, and it was as well that it did not." A fall from an upper yard meant almost certain death, and the wonder is that more sailors were not lost this way.

British writer Eric Newby, who left an advertising agency to serve as an apprentice, later wrote about working in a furious wind with several other crewmen to furl a topsail of the four-masted bark *Moshulu* in a raging South Pacific storm. Suddenly he found himself falling. "I was the last man out on the weather side and was engaged in casting loose a gasket before we started to work on the sail, when without warning it flicked up, forty feet of canvas as hard as corrugated iron, and knocked me clean off the footrope. There was no interval for reflection, no sudden upsurge of remorse for past sins, nor did my life pass in rapid review before my eyes. Instead there was a delightful jerk, and I found myself entangled in the weather rigging some five feet below the yard, and as soon as I could, I climbed back to the yard and carried on with my job. I felt no fear at all until much later on."

Newby's companions were too busy to notice what had happened. Back on deck, one of them, a Finn, noticed that Newby looked a bit shaken and asked if something had gone wrong. "I fell," said Newby. "I din see," said the other. "I don' believe."

There were many ways besides falling for a seaman to get hurt furling sail. Villiers recalled a desperate fight to bring in a topsail on the *Herzogin Cecilie*, all the men exhausted, their hands "blue with cold and red with blood," as the 2,000-square-foot canvas kept eluding them. "Once a steel bunt line, writhing back over the yard, caught Zimmerman in the head and brought the swift blood. He reeled a bit, but carried on. Then after a while we saw that he had fainted, and lay in imminent peril across the yard. For one awful moment the canvas stayed still while we fought to him, and then because we could not take him down we lashed him there. And when we had time to remember him again we found that he had come to, and was working."

The worst of it was that, even in only moderately severe weather, furling and unfurling sail had to be done over and over again. As the wind picked up or slackened, the amount of canvas a ship could safely carry would change, and a captain would always try to keep as much sail set as he prudently could. He kept a close eye on the barometer and

The ultimate windships

Full-rigged windjammers flew more canvas than any other ships. The four-masted German bark *Herzogin Cecilie*, with 34 sails bent to the wind, boasted a total sail area of almost 45,000 square feet, more than an acre of canvas. This awesome spread of sail soared more than 150 feet above the deck, and the foresail alone measured 87 by 33 feet.

Yet for all the complexity of a windjammer's top-hamper, it was designed to follow some of the most elementary tenets of sailing. For the main drive, three great masts carried 18 square sails—canvases cut shallow but broad, to offer both ease in handling and the maximum surface area to the wind. Set on sturdy yards, some more than 90 feet long, these square sails could be braced perpendicularly to the keel to make the most of a following wind, or they could be hauled in close.

In addition to square sails, a ship like the *Herzogin Ceci-*

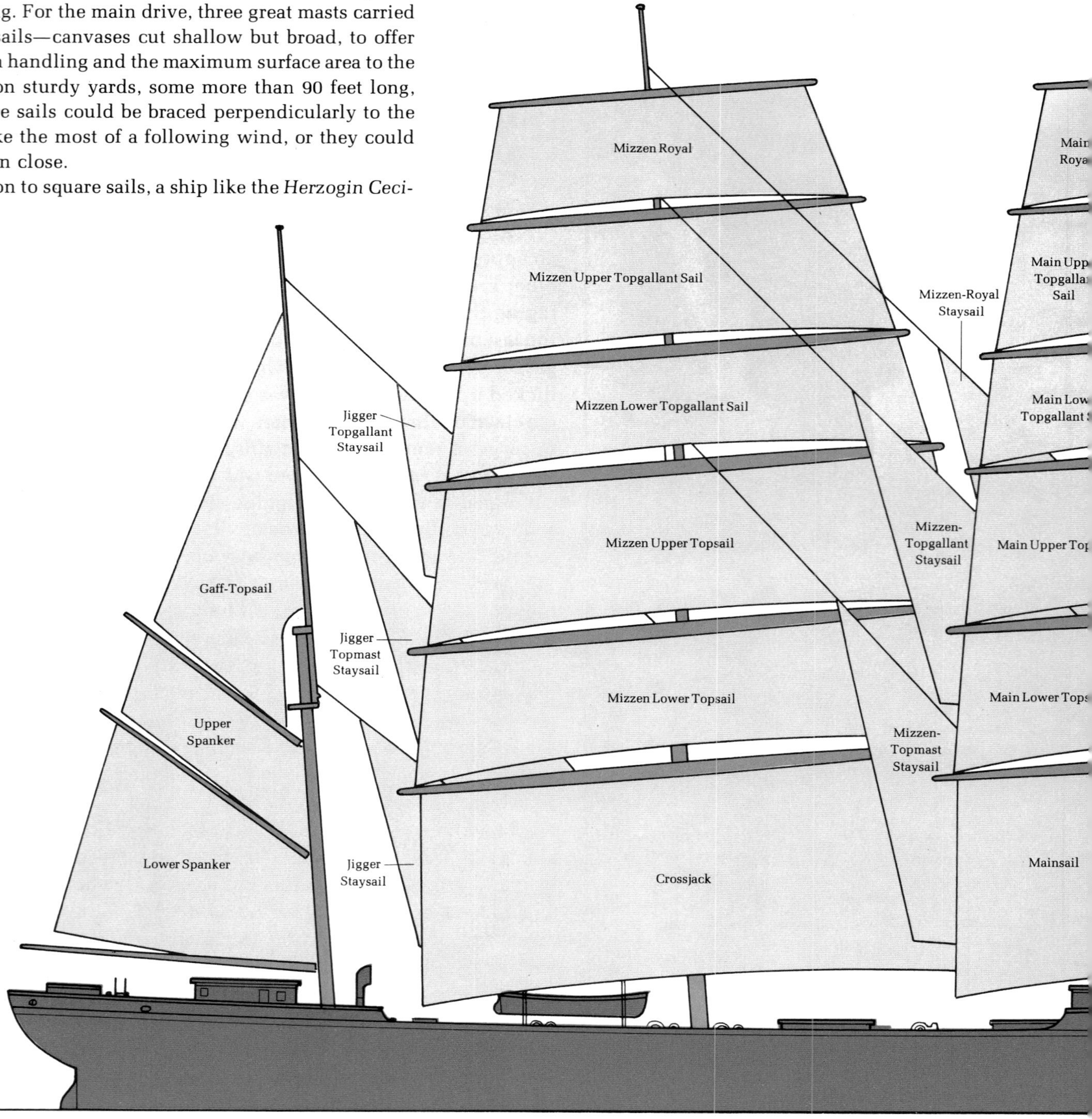

Mizzen Royal

Mizzen Upper Topgallant Sail

Mizzen Lower Topgallant Sail

Mizzen Upper Topsail

Mizzen Lower Topsail

Crossjack

Mizzen-Royal Staysail

Mizzen-Topgallant Staysail

Mizzen-Topmast Staysail

Main Royal

Main Upper Topgallant Sail

Main Lower Topgallant Sail

Main Upper Topsail

Main Lower Topsail

Mainsail

Jigger Topgallant Staysail

Jigger Topmast Staysail

Jigger Staysail

Gaff-Topsail

Upper Spanker

Lower Spanker

lie often carried 16 or more triangular sails rigged fore and aft. Although smaller, these sails could hold a better angle to the wind than the square sails, providing an important boost when the ship edged up into the wind. This was the main function of the triangular staysails between the masts. In the bow the triangular jibs and fore-topmast staysail were vital steering sails. Filled, these headsails turned the bow away from the wind, aiding the helmsman when he altered course to leeward.

In the stern the spankers and the gaff-topsail provided an opposite force, pressing the stern away from the wind. To keep a steady course, the fore-and-aft sails would offset each other while still contributing to the forward drive. To alter course, the captain could upset these balanced forces on the jibs and spankers to use the power of the wind, as well as that of his rudder, to turn his mammoth ship.

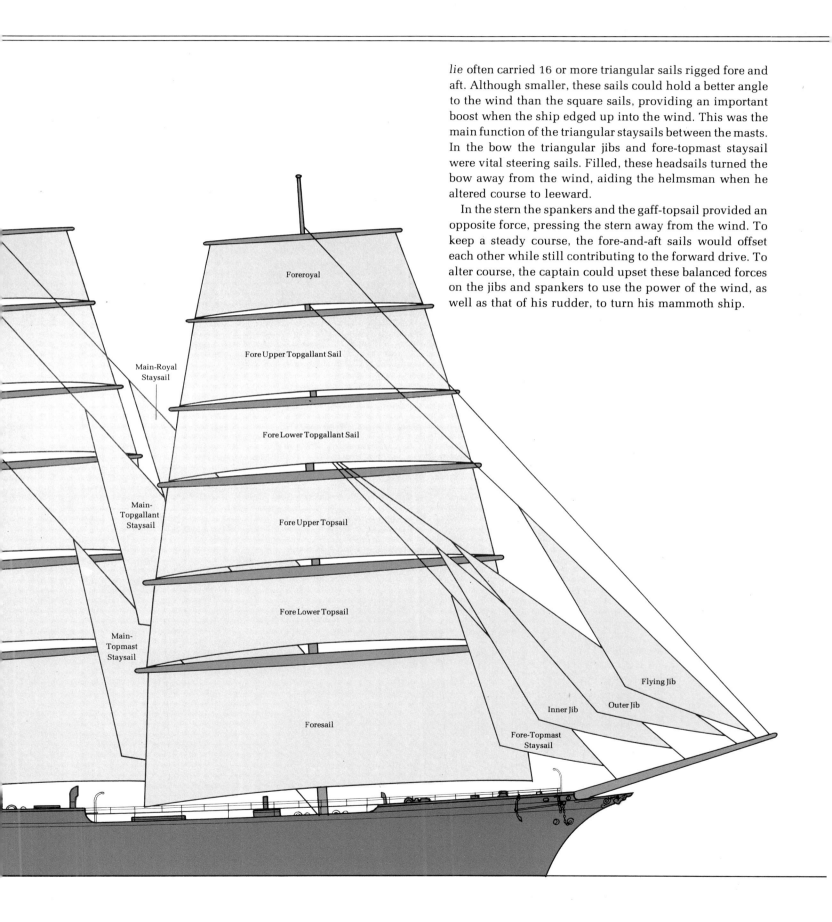

Foreroyal

Fore Upper Topgallant Sail

Main-Royal
Staysail

Fore Lower Topgallant Sail

Main-
Topgallant
Staysail

Fore Upper Topsail

Fore Lower Topsail

Main-
Topmast
Staysail

Flying Jib

Inner Jib

Outer Jib

Foresail

Fore-Topmast
Staysail

Matching canvas to the fury of the elements

The strength and direction of wind and seas, the particular handling characteristics of the ship, the distribution of cargo weight, the size of the crew, even the personality of the captain—all these factors determined a windjammer's sail load. The *Herzogin Cecilie* could at times carry her full suit of 35 sails in winds up to 40 knots.

In higher winds, however, excess canvas threatened the stability and even the survival of the ship. Caught unpre-pared by a storm, an overcanvased vessel could be dismast-ed, knocked over on her beam-ends or literally driven un-derwater by a following wind—although more often her sails would simply blow out, leaving only tattered rags on the yards. To avoid such disaster, most shipmasters pru-dently reduced sail as the force of a storm intensified, fol-lowing a systematic procedure similar to the one used on the *Herzogin Cecilie*, shown below.

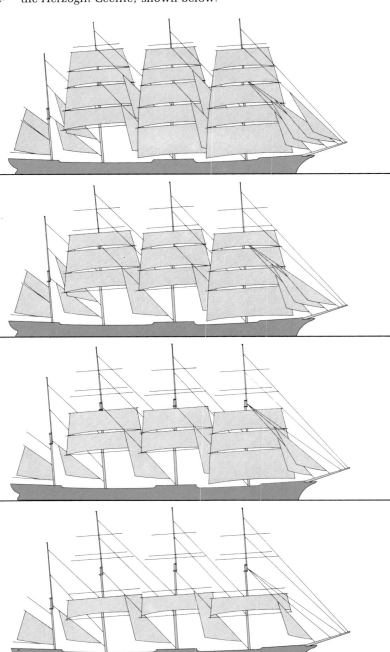

When the wind rose above 40 knots, the first sails to be taken in were the uppermost sails—the royals, upper staysails and gaff-topsail aft—and the huge crossjack, set at the bottom of the mizzenmast. The furling of these sails reduced mounting wind pressure on the masts. With the wind abeam, these sails tended to list the vessel, which increased drag on the hull and negated any speed the sails added.

In a strong gale—i.e., one approaching 50 knots—sail was reduced even more by furling the great mainsail, set at the bottom of the mainmast. Then a few hands took in the flying jib, while the rest of the crew climbed aloft to furl the next-highest line of sails, the topgallants and the topgallant staysails. Though now carrying scarcely half her sails, the ship could still make good headway in such winds.

If the wind continued to rise toward 60 knots, again the highest line of sails was furled—this time the upper topsails. With these large square sails secure, the crew dropped the outer jib in the bow and two small fore-and-aft sails in the stern. By now, decks would be awash as the ship beat to windward, and headway would be greatly reduced by heavy seas.

The last great sail, the foresail, was not furled until the wind approached 70 knots. Then came the inner jib, leaving only the lower spanker, the lowest staysails and the lower topsails to drive the ship ahead. In winds of more than 80 knots, the ship often hove to with mizzen lower topsail furled, keeping her bow to the wind with the other seven sails still flying.

shortened down when the weather was likely to worsen, then put out more canvas again when things improved. It was not at all unusual for a crew to spend an entire day struggling to take in a dozen or more sails, only to discover later in the evening that the storm was abating, and to be ordered aloft once more to break out every sail the ship could carry. And sails had a way of breaking loose. "On the main upper tops'l," recalled one seaman, "we was laying with 24 men—even the cook was up there for eight hours trying to make it fast. Well, we had that sail in and then we got tired and then the wind came and it blew out again. We was up there from midnight until seven in the morning until we had it fast at last."

After hours of bone-chilling work, the men would fall into their wet bunks still dressed in their oilskins and drop off to sleep almost instantly. But they were always subject to call—at a summons from the mate's whistle they would have to tumble out at any time, day or night, and clamber aloft.

When the wind shifted direction, the crew would turn to another part of the running rigging—the braces, which controlled the angle of the yards and sails. Those ropes or wires ran from the ends of the yards down to the deck—to Jarvis winches if a ship was fortunate enough to have them. Proper bracing of the yards would allow a windjammer to sail surprisingly close to the direction from which the wind was coming. Clumsy though their rig might look, most windjammers could sail within six points of the wind—that is, they could make good a course that came close to 60° of the wind's direction. And a few could do even better. The four-masted French bark *Nord* was reputed to be able to sail five points (56¼°) from the wind.

Bracing the yards required precise timing and coordination: while the windward braces were being paid out, the lee braces were being taken in. And like everything else on a windjammer, it was heavy work, especially when the yards had to be squared—hauled back against the force of the wind until they were at right angles to the ship's axis. Where the wind was steady, as in the trades of the South Atlantic, the yards might be braced only once or twice a day, but in some areas it was almost nonstop work, especially in the doldrums near the equator, where light breezes might come up from one quarter, vanish, and then reappear suddenly from another.

When a square-rigger was sailing before the wind, bracing the yards was a simple matter. When she was sailing into the wind, the yards had to be adjusted to allow the sails to catch the maximum amount of air without being taken aback—catching the wind on the wrong side and being blown back against the masts, a situation that could lead to dismasting in a strong blow. In his effort to steer "full and by"—that is, to hold the ship as close to the wind as possible while still keeping the sails full—the helmsman was aided by yards braced to set the ship's sails in a slight corkscrew pattern. The yard for the lowest sail, known as the course, was braced around as far as it would go, pointing the sail as high as possible into the wind. Each higher yard was brought around slightly less, its sail filling more easily because it was turned at more of an angle to the wind. The helmsman kept his eye on the mizzen royal's weather edge. If it started to flutter, or luff, he knew he was coming up into the wind too much and must ease off. When that sail was just full, all the others would surely draw well. When running before a strong wind, a well-designed ship would almost steer herself.

Yet sooner or later, no matter how well she was going, a ship would have to be tacked, her bow swung across the wind and her sails trimmed to take the wind as it came across the other side of the ship (page 34). For it was only by tacking—zigzagging back and forth in the general direction from which the wind was coming—that a ship could work its way toward an upwind destination.

Even under the best of circumstances, tacking a windjammer required thorough preparation and precision of execution; it called for all the accumulated skills of captain and crew. The process was always directed personally by the captain, who stood by the helmsman and shouted his orders to the mates.

Eric Newby remembers the maneuver as executed on the *Moshulu*. The ship had been sailing outbound from Belfast to Port Lincoln, South Australia, on a starboard tack—the wind coming across the starboard bow. Even though she would soon be swung to starboard, into the wind, the captain's first order took her the other way. "Keep her clean full," he shouted, and she was eased off a bit from the wind so that she could pick up speed. She would need it. "Ready about!" called the captain.

Now his crew was alert for quick action. "Down helm!" he called. The helmsman spun the wheel hard and the *Moshulu* began turning into the wind, her canvas flapping, her rigging shaking. Men stationed aft heaved at a sail called the spanker to help push the stern around. Those forward would let fly the jib to allow the bow to come into the wind. As the massive *Moshulu*—3,116 tons, 335 feet long—turned, she also, inevitably, lost headway. For a few moments, all her sails were aback; if some of them were not braced around immediately to catch the wind from the port side, she would be in irons—wallowing bow to the breeze, with no headway whatsoever.

Timing was vital. "Mainsail haul!" called the captain. That was the traditional command for hauling the main and mizzen yards around. Chanting, every muscle straining, the men working the winches and lines canted the yards to catch the wind from a new slant. The move was well timed and the yards came around easily, helped by the wind. As they did, their sails began filling and the *Moshulu* began to regain steerage way. Now the sails on the mainmast and mizzenmast pushed the stern in one direction while those on the foremast, still aback, were pushing in the other direction, helping to keep the ship turning during the final phase of the tacking maneuver.

As the ship neared her new course, the captain watched her closely. At the precise moment that he yelled "Let go and haul!" the crew raced forward to swing the foreyards around to the same angle as those on the mainmast and mizzenmast.

Now all the sails and yards could be given their proper trim. All lines were coiled or otherwise arranged for quick handling when the ship would have to swing back to the starboard tack—as the *Moshulu* did soon enough. When it was over, recalled Newby, "I had never been so

Tacking through the wind

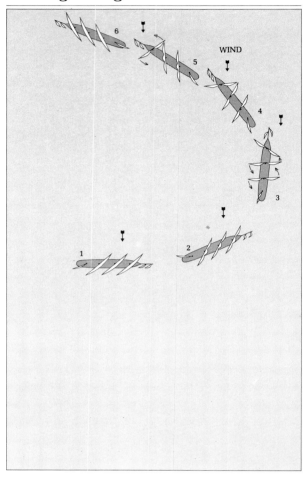

The fastest and most efficient way for a windjammer captain to change course was to tack, bringing the bow across the wind. (1) Sailing on a port tack, the ship was allowed to fall off away from the wind. (2) The helm was put over hard to port, and the spanker sail was hauled to windward to pivot the ship. (3) The main and mizzen yards were braced around: their sails and the jibs fluttered for a moment while the wind struck the front of the foresails, driving the ship to port. (4) The ship rapidly lost momentum, but as she came around, the jibs and the mainsail and mizzen sail filled. (5) As the vessel gained way again, the foreyards were braced around to the new course. (6) With the ship picking up speed, all sails were trimmed for the starboard tack.

Wearing around the wind

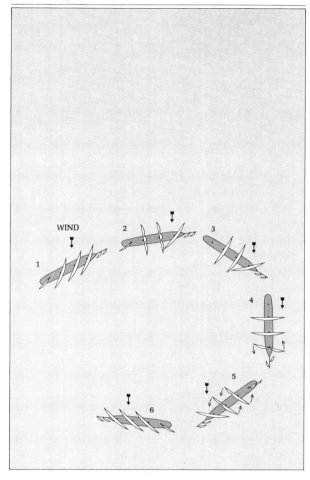

WIND

1 2 3 4 5 6

Wearing ship, altering course by bringing the vessel's stern across the wind, was a maneuver used primarily in heavy weather. (1) Under reduced sail, the ship was readied for a run downwind. (2) The spanker was furled, and the rudder was put over to starboard while the mainsail and mizzen sail were squared into the wind. (3) The ship fell off to leeward until the wind aft filled the main and mizzen. (4) With the wind directly astern, the main and mizzen blanketed the forward sails, freeing them to be hauled around for the starboard tack. (5) The forward sails filled, and the main and mizzen were braced around farther to take the wind over the starboard side. (6) Having reversed direction, the ship was trimmed for the new course and the spanker was reset.

tired in my whole life, far too exhausted to appreciate the beautiful pyramids of sail towering above me."

How long it might take to tack varied widely depending on sea and wind conditions. With a good breeze to help her pick up speed at the start of a tack and then push her around smartly, a windjammer could be tacked in as little as 15 minutes. But in light airs it could take as long as an hour or more for her to come around. Equally troublesome was extremely heavy weather, which sometimes made it too dangerous even to attempt a tack. In that case, the only way to change an upwind course was by wearing ship, a procedure under which the vessel was turned not into the wind but away from it and on through a complete circle until she was on her new course *(page 35)*. Wearing ship was safer than tacking, for the sails were not taken aback, but it lost time and distance. All skippers tacked whenever possible.

Whether a ship was beating into the wind with frequent tacks or running before it for long miles, standing a trick at the wheel when things were going well could be immensely satisfying. "The feel of the ship completely under the control of my own hands," wrote one sailor, "her lofty masts towering above with their wide spreads of canvas silhouetted against the star-studded tropic sky, every one of the 24 sails straining in the comfortably stiff breeze, the slap and swish of the water as we glided along at a ten-knot clip, steering full-and-by—it all sent a quivering, excited thrill through me."

Heavy weather meant much heavier work at the wheel. Sometimes it took four men on a double-wheeled vessel to fight the wave pressure against a windjammer's massive rudder. A sudden lurch, a loosened hold on the wheel's spinning spokes, and a helmsman could be flipped across the deck. One veteran recalled trying to stop the wheel from spinning by pressing it with his arm. His elbow caught a spoke, and he was flipped athwart ship into the rail. The spoke broke off; he kept it as a memento.

Wind and wave were not the only elements affecting a vessel's steering characteristics. Each one had her own idiosyncrasies; the placement of her masts, the cut of her sails, some slight quirk in the shape of her hull could make her perform differently from sister ships. Carelessly loaded cargo could unbalance the hardiest ship and turn her into a ponderous hulk. Worse yet, cargo could shift in a storm. When that happened, so much weight might move that a ship could be thrown on her beamends—she would roll over on her side with her yardarms touching the water. If the ship did not recover swiftly, water could surge through hatch coverings and cause her to founder.

When the four-masted bark *Bengairn* was caught in a nasty shift of wind in late 1907 off the Australian coast and her coal cargo shifted to one side, she rolled over and the sea poured through one of her hatches. Working with desperate speed, her crew stretched a brand-new topsail over the hatch to stem the flow of water. Then they got rid of the upper masts and yards—the so-called top-hamper—by cutting shrouds and stays and allowing them to fall into the sea. Some 80 tons of metal went into the water. Her center of gravity lowered, the ship rolled back a bit. Only then could the crew begin hauling the coal back into place. Shovel-

Dead reckoning: a navigator's salvation in heavy weather

While a crewman holds a sandglass, an officer gauges the speed of his ship by counting the knots unreeling on a log line.

Every windjammer master carried a chronometer and marine sextant so he could fix his position at sea by sighting the sun and the stars, but these sophisticated devices were often useless in the turbulent Southern latitudes, where the skies all too often were obscured day and night by thick masses of storm clouds. On some days, in the blowing sleet, rain or snow, even the horizon would be obscured from view.

Yet so long as a master could determine his speed and compass course, he could, after making an educated guess about current and drift, calculate his position with reasonable accuracy by simple arithmetic. This navigational technique was called dead reckoning, from old seamen's usage. And for many a sailing master, it was the only thing that stood between him and calamity.

Keeping track of the vessel's compass course was no problem in all but the stormiest conditions. But judging speed through the water was some-

thing else again. Ancient mariners estimated speed by timing how long it took the ship to pass by a chip, or log, cast in the water from the bow: if it took 10 seconds for a 100-foot ship to pass, she was making 600 feet per minute, or 36,000 feet per hour, which

Walker's distance-recording log consisted of a finned metal "log" (below) that rotated when towed astern of a ship, and a register dial on board (right), which translated the revolutions of the log into nautical miles. The recorder was nicknamed "cherub," possibly in salute to the device as a guardian angel.

came to roughly six nautical miles.

By the early days of the windjammers, ship speed was computed with a log line—a reeled-up line, knotted at even intervals and tied at one end to a log, or float. At a signal from the watch officer, the log was streamed overboard for an exact period of time, measured by turning a sandglass, while a seaman counted the number of knots unreeled on the line. The distance between the knots on the line bore the same relation to a nautical mile as the turning of the glass bore to one hour.

"Reeling off the knots" became a tradition at sea, and a smart day's run was a matter of great pride to windjammer crews. Yet the log-line readings, taken only once each watch, were open to distortion over long voyages.

By 1900 most windjammers were equipped with a distance-recording log (*below*), which eliminated measuring knots altogether. Patented by British manufacturer Thomas Walker in 1878, the log could be towed astern for the entire voyage. By registering the nautical miles a ship had run, the log gave a master precise distance readings from which he could figure his ship's position.

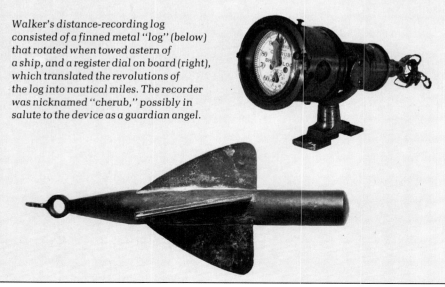

ing it was impossible—it slid right back. Tackles were rigged to move it in baskets. For days everyone—captain, mates, seamen—worked in what they remembered as the "terrible, dusty, heaving gloom" to shift the coal, while the pumps gradually got rid of the water. In time, still listing badly, the *Bengairn* sailed under stump masts to Sydney, where she had to be taken in tow to an anchorage. And that, quite likely, was the most embarrassing part of the voyage for the *Bengairn's* unhappy captain and crew. To a windjammer man the very idea of being hauled around by a chuffing, smoking little tug was anathema. It was obviously necessary, of course, when entering a narrow, twisting harbor channel or when shunting around a congested harbor. But whenever and wherever humanly possible the windjammers did things on their own.

The sight of a great four-master sweeping into harbor, with all sails set, maneuvering under perfect control, was a spectacle that no one who had witnessed it, seaman or landlubber, was ever likely to forget. A flawless demonstration by the German *Lisbeth* in a port in Chile during the early years of the 20th Century could still be recalled in every detail years later by an observer:

"Tocopilla Bay forms the segment of a circle, with a bluff headland at its northern extremity and an ugly reef of rocks stretching out to seaward from its southern end. The ships in port lay in a single tier, reaching from close under the lee of the reef to within a quarter of a mile of the headland, and at no great distance from the shore.

"One afternoon we saw a bark not far out in the offing standing boldly into the anchorage with every stitch of canvas set. She was heading straight in for the line of shipping before the town and coming along grandly, leaning steeply over, with a flashing bow-wave curling away on either side of her. To an onlooker from the port, it appeared as though she were determined to pile herself up.

"On she came, with never a sheet or a tack started. The men on the nearest ship ran out, thinking there would be a collision. The bark still came on, with no sign of shortening sail. Only, as she approached, she was observed to alter course slightly in order to head between the endmost vessel and the headland. It was magnificent, or monstrous foolhardiness, just precisely which was not apparent.

"The stranger stood unwaveringly in till she was within a few hundred yards of the nearest ship, and not more than a cable's length from the headland. Then we heard a whistle aboard her. Down went her helm, hard-a-port, topsail and topgallant halliards whined in the sheaves, staysail hanks tinkled swiftly down the stays, and the bark swept boldly down under the stern of the anchored shipping. With lessening momentum she stood straight down the narrow fairway between them and the shore. A minute or two more, and she ported again. Then, passing between the end ship and the southern reef, with her bows pointing fair out to sea, and her men furling sail like heroes, she let go her anchor and brought up, in the best berth in the harbor."

Showmanship? No doubt. But that performance also took skill and nerve. It took men of singular devotion to sail, tough men with pride in great, powerful ships of swift, high loveliness that has not been matched since windjammers passed from the seas.

Chapter 2

Lordly masters of all they surveyed

eter John Riber Mathieson, of Viking blood and British birthright, later a Canadian citizen and finally an American, was born in the cabin of his father's trim little wooden bark, the *Haakon Jarl*, anchored at Gravesend, while the wind blew strong and fair. During his long deepwater life, he served before and abaft the mast, under sail and with steam, on 41 vessels carrying the flags of six nations. In 1944, as master of the American steamer *Joseph E. Wing*, Mathieson survived attack from Japanese aircraft, unloaded high explosives at Morotai in the Molucca Islands, and then retired to Montreal—at age 73.

Dearest to him of all his ships was the full-rigged iron windjammer *Antiope*, built in 1866 in Scotland to carry mixed cargo to Australia and the Orient. To some, she was a jinx ship—called the *Anti-Hope*, partly in an obvious play on her name, partly in dark recognition that during her days she suffered a mutiny (not under Mathieson), was seized by the Japanese Navy (during the Russo-Japanese War in 1905), and was once taken aground and stranded for 96 days before being refloated. But to Mathieson, who came to captain her when she was carrying salt in 1905, she was "my lovely vessel" and "brave old *Antiope*." And as he well knew, "No matter what befell her, she always pulled through."

Her captain polished the teakwood of her saloon with a mixture of olive oil and lime juice, which made it gleaming and fragrant. He related how he fitted the airy room out with "a couple of fine rugs on the deck, a grand piano, settees, chairs and tables, flowers growing in boxes, and canaries hanging in cages in the big skylight." Mathieson gloried in the *Antiope*'s grace: "She seemed," he wrote, "to be almost alive, running clean and strong, the sails pulling for all they were worth. No smoke. No dust. No noise. Nothing but the music of wind and sea."

On the night of November 11, 1906, the *Antiope* seemed about to die. The evening started out "ugly, menacing, and black as a pocket," Mathieson later recalled. The *Antiope* had been caught by a gale in the South Pacific between the Tonga Islands and North Cape, New Zealand, and as Mathieson clung to the poop rail he had "a strange sense of foreboding that the howling wind and snarling sea were in collusion and had picked the *Antiope* for a victim." Still, as the evil evening passed, there was little change—the weather was no better, but no worse—and Mathieson went below for a catnap. Suddenly he "felt the vessel shudder violently, a terrible wrenching back-breaking shudder."

Even as he rushed for the chartroom stairs, Mathieson realized what had happened: the *Antiope* had been taken aback. She had been making a south-southeast course under gale-force northwest winds, which, unforeseen and unforeseeable, had shifted a full 90° into the southwest and were now pounding the ship from ahead.

The *Antiope* had not been rigged for such treatment: she was set up to take the wind from behind, and now her headstays were in torment. If they gave way, masts and yards would surely come crashing down, maiming and killing, and the *Antiope*, helpless, could be driven stern first into her own grave.

Mathieson would remember the scene to the end of his days: "The wind, blowing hard from right ahead. The rain a wild rushing down-

Captain Alexander Teschner—20 years a ship's master for the German firm of Laeisz—serenely nurses a pipe as he stands in his oilskins by the wheel of the rain-washed Pera in 1901. Masters like Teschner had the authority of absolute monarchs. But the best captains exercised their power judiciously. "They were quiet-spoken, clean-living men, though they could make noise enough when it was necessary," recalled one Cape Horner.

pour. The sea a grey-green roaring menace. And the *Antiope* tearing stern first through the raging waters." He struggled toward the helmsman, and in the next few moments showed his mettle as a master. He shouted against the wind's scream: "Ease helm amidship! Slow! Spoke by spoke!" The helmsman obeyed, bringing the rudder to a neutral position so that the ship, while being thrust back, would not turn out of control. "Now port!" Mathieson ordered, once she had steadied, seeking to bring her gently around to a northerly course with the wind at her stern. "Half! Slow! Careful! Lose your hold and we lose the rudder!" At that instant an oil lamp in the chartroom shook loose from its bracket and smashed onto the floor, rapidly spreading flames. "Get a rug!" cried Mathieson to a cabin boy. "Quick! Smother the flames!"—whereupon the lad fainted dead away.

Then the *Antiope* pooped. "She seemed to fall backward," recalled Mathieson. "Down! Down! Down! Into the hungry clutch of the great grey-beard racing up and on." Yet that monstrous wave brought salvation. Surging around the shoulders of the men clinging for their lives to the mizzen rigging, it buried the poop, crashed through the chartroom door and poured tons of water onto the gathering fire, putting it out.

"Wheel amidships!" shouted Mathieson as the *Antiope* slowly came about, stern first, her sails beginning to fill. The *Antiope* gained headway, and Mathieson gave the order signifying that the worst was past: "Keep her full and bye!" Then, in perhaps the proudest moment of John Mathieson's life, cheers came from the crew: "Hurrah, *Antiope!*"

The whole episode had lasted less than 12 minutes. Yet in that terrifying flicker of time, Mathieson had kept his head. He had relied upon instinct and drawn from experience. He had given the right orders at precisely the right time. He had saved his ship. And in so doing, he had performed in the highest tradition of the tall ships' masters.

The master, Mathieson once wrote, was "lord of all he surveyed, his vessel, and all those in her under his immediate command, and the whole open sea before him on which to shape his course. He had to be a little of everything—sailor, navigator, carpenter, sailmaker, meteorologist, lawyer, and doctor, and able to read the burial service. When in port, he had to contend with all those who made their living from shipping: the ship chandler, the butcher, the stevedore, the dry-dock people, and had to know how to deal with the agent, the consignee, the customs officials, the shipping master, and the port officials. He had to collect the money for the freight, pay all expenses, keep all accounts and send the balance of the freight money to his owners with a statement of accounts. I performed all these duties and received a salary of $100 per month."

As disparate as the talents they were called upon to command were the windjammer masters themselves. Men of many nations, habits and temperaments, they offered no tidy formula for success, or even for survival in their perilous profession. Yet when the day of the windjammer came to wane, certain names were repeatedly mentioned wherever veterans of the tall ships gathered to talk of departed shipmates and forgotten islands and barren nitrate coasts and the keen of the gale off the Horn.

A composite of greatness may be drawn from the individual qualities

Awesome conditions of command

"Old Man Captain de Cloux," recalled a sailor who served under him in the 1920s, "remembers nothing about the ports he has seen, except perhaps the excessive cost of discharging there or an extortionate bill for the coal supply of the ship's galley."

And no wonder. For the captain of a windjammer was a shipowner's sole agent in most foreign ports, and on his shoulders rested the responsibility for the voyage's profit or loss. In some cases, a captain's bargain with the owner was sealed simply by a handshake. But the wisest course, followed by captains like de Cloux and by the firms for which they worked, was to spell everything out in a written contract. Thus both parties knew exactly what was expected and what the captain's recompense would be.

Contracts varied widely, depending on the wealth of the company and on the eminence of the captain. But generally the owners paid the captain a modest monthly salary—and added a percentage of the cargo's value, which might make him rich. In return, the owners made a remarkable, even awesome, number of demands on the captain in order to assert their control over an operation thousands of miles from home.

A typical contract signed at Nantes, France, in 1904 between the Nantes Sailing Ship Co. Ltd. and Captain A. Bidon, who was appointed to command its vessel *Amiral de Cornulier*, stipulated:

The captain should monitor his stowing; he should watch out and count the number of bags of cargo well.

The ship being sufficiently equipped with cordage,

and careers of five remarkable captains: C. C. (he always went by his initials) Dixon, a doughty Nova Scotian who was jack-of-all-skills and master of most; James Learmont, a Scotsman of unswerving honesty who drove fast ships and hard bargains; W. S. Leask, also a Scotsman but of rougher cut, as canny in his business dealings as he was uncanny in his seafaring instincts; Robert Hilgendorf, a German whose eerie way with the wind made lesser men believe him to be allied with the devil; and Robert Miethe, another German, the last great captain of the five-masted barks, sturdy and tough as a stanchion yet possessed of a tender love for the great ships he sailed and served.

If, as Mathieson said, diversity was the hallmark of the windjammer master, then the extraordinary little Bluenoser (as Nova Scotians were called), C. C. Dixon, holds rank in the deepwater pantheon. In addition to possessing all the skills and qualities enumerated by Mathieson, Dixon was an enthusiastic inventor, surveyor, explorer, photographer, oceanographer, ornithologist, ichthyologist, geologist and debunker of myths about the sea.

Waves towering 100 feet high? Nonsense. Dixon had measured and photographed them in all parts of the world and "they were not half that height." Sharks always turn over on their backs to bite? "That," said Dixon, who had observed them long and carefully, "is not the case at all." Sharks could and did bite with awful effectiveness right side up. Cape Horn waters frozen into ice floes? Dixon sailed the Horn 16 times and took readings on every passage; the lowest temperature he ever recorded was 32½° F. Derelict ships and skeleton crews caught in the morass of the Sargasso Sea? Dixon towed a net for two nautical miles through the weediest area, and came up with only 16 pounds of weeds.

These quiddities aside, Dixon was a superb mariner who, by his own meticulous reckoning, during his 30 years at sea had sailed precisely 1,007,208 miles. On a number of occasions his broad knowledge and ingenuity were all that pulled him and his crew out of a nasty situation. On one passage from Rotterdam to Portland, Oregon, the mate responsible for rationing fresh water squandered it until, as Dixon recalled, "there wasn't enough left to wash a shirt with." The crew faced death from thirst until Dixon rigged a contraption that boiled sea water and condensed the steam; he got 15 gallons of fresh distilled water a day from it, enough for their needs.

Of all the passages, none was more testing of Dixon's endless ingenuity than a 14,000-mile race from Sydney around the Horn to the Strait of Dover that began in April 1907. The contest, like most, began with a boast. Dixon's vessel at the time was the full-rigged *Arctic Stream*. Lying near her in Sydney Harbor was the four-masted German training bark *Herzogin Sophie Charlotte*. As his departure time neared, the German captain, in what Dixon clearly considered to be a crass piece of showboating, announced that the *Herzogin Sophie Charlotte* would clear the congested harbor under her own sail, without help from tugs. "It didn't lie well on my stomach," Dixon recalled. "I had been brought up in Nova Scotia and I thought then, as I do now, that a Nova Scotia skipper can do as much with a ship as any man afloat. In a shipping office one morning,

---

sailcloths, rope, etc., no purchase of these supplies should be made except in a case of absolute necessity and with the authorization of the shipping firm.

No private cargoes should be taken on by the captain without having previously had the authorization of his shipping firm for each voyage.

A book of expenditure mentioning all the provisions loaded on board the ship is provided by the shipping firm to the captain at the beginning of the voyage. An exact copy of the book should be sent from each port to the shipping firm, and upon returning to Europe, the book should be handed over.

Upon his arrival in a port, the captain should himself telegraph his arrival. During his stay he should give regularly, by departing ship or wireless, a report on his operations, taking care to note the dates on which the time for unloading or loading begins and ends, while giving all the explanatory information on the delays that might occur.

The ship's log is recorded by the captain himself, who should relate there all the accidents and incidents of the crossing; he should send a copy of it to his shipping firm on his arrival at each port.

Upon arriving in Europe, the captain should establish a complete inventory of the equipment.

Woe betide the sloppy or inconstant skipper. One captain returned to Dieppe with a cargo that was found short of what was on the manifest. The man had to pay a 15,000-franc fine, nearly wiping out his commission from the arduous months-long voyage.

I said I could make the *Arctic Stream* of Glasgow do anything the German ship could do, and probably a bit more, if I crowded my men.''

Such challenges do not pass unheeded on the world's waterfronts. ''Before I could turn around,'' said Dixon, ''bets were flying, and I had agreed to race the German ship to the Strait of Dover.'' *The Sydney Morning Herald* expressed the prevailing view of the probable outcome: ''The commander of the *Arctic Stream*, a typical Canadian, claims that his vessel has never been beaten when matched for a trial of speed. The German training ship has a reputation for smart sailing, and on one occasion completed the run from Melbourne to Bremen in 76 days. It is doubtful whether the *Arctic Stream* has ever matched herself against a vessel of such fine sailing qualities, and the *Herzogin Sophie Charlotte* is therefore the favourite.''

There were moments in the days that followed when Dixon must have regretted his cockiness. The *Arctic Stream* was sailing full-loaded, with a cargo of shale, while the big German bark was much less heavily burdened. Dixon had a mixed-bag crew of 24 and the *Herzogin Sophie*

Perched nonchalantly on the bowsprit, Captain and Mrs. Pierre Stephan enjoy a honeymoon in 1905 on the French windjammer President Felix Faure, bound for New Caledonia. As a welcome to Mrs. Stephan, the firm of Brown and Corblet stocked the ship with canned delicacies and champagne. The provisions were also a reward for the 24-year-old captain, who earlier that year had sailed the crippled ship across the Atlantic, though she was taking on up to 100 tons of water a day through a loose hull plate.

Charlotte was manned by 80 smartly trained cadets. To make matters worse, the *Herzogin Sophie Charlotte* got a three-day head start, cleared the harbor under sail just as her captain had promised and was making 12 knots in ideal weather conditions as she swept through Sydney Heads. "I don't think you'll catch that fellow, Captain," said an onlooker as Dixon watched the German depart. Replied Dixon, with more confidence than he felt: "It's a long way to the Strait of Dover." Still, he grudgingly admitted that "the German ship did indeed look impressive as she surged out to the open sea."

For the *Arctic Stream* the journey began as if she were bewitched. Day after maddening day the winds were light and variable. Dixon was hard put to make 200 miles during each 24-hour period. Then, as the *Arctic Stream* approached Cape Horn, the wind picked up and held steady. Dixon piled on sail—in his words, "I put out all our washing"—and was coursing along, hoping to gain on the Germans, when came the dire cry: "Man overboard!" A sailor named Jan Johannsen had been clearing the foresheet when suddenly he had yelled and tumbled into the sea. Dixon instantly brought the *Arctic Stream* about and searched the area for hours. But no sign of the man could be found. At last Dixon entered the circumstances of death in his log, turned and headed back on course.

Dixon's troubles were just starting. Now, as the Horn drew close, the wind rose to hurricane force in the night, great "graybeards," as cascading waves were called, poured over the ship's rails, the masts trembled and the *Arctic Stream* shuddered as she fought the seas. "I don't think she'll stand much more o' this, sir," said the mate. "She can stand a lot of this," replied Dixon—even as a telltale shriek from the darkness aloft gave grim announcement that one of the topsails had split. "Better heave to, before the other goes, sir," shouted the mate. But little Dixon was all grit. "She'll run all right, even if the second one does go," he said. "I've seen her run under bare sticks before, in a worse sea than this."

Yet as the murderous tempest rose, with snow piling into the rigging and waves drowning the ship in six feet of water, even Dixon decided that to take in his remaining topsail was the better part of valor. For more than an hour, said Dixon, the crew was aloft "struggling with the threshing, ice-coated canvas, and hanging on with their teeth and toenails." At last the job was done. Even under bare poles, Dixon related, "without a stitch of canvas on her, the ship was doing twelve knots."

Still, one crisis was followed by another, often even more deadly. Without sail, burdened by tons of water, buffeted by massive seas, the ship began to lose control. And somewhere just ahead lay the Diego Ramírez Islands, 60 miles southwest of the Horn, the last visible outcroppings of the Andes, with jagged cliffs rising 200 feet from the sea and concealed behind clouds of spray thrown up by the waves that crashed against them.

It was time and past time for the resourceful Dixon to reach into his seabag of tricks. "I think a little oil would take the tops off these seas," he said to the mate. "Better try it." Two buckets of fish oil, ordinarily used for rigging maintenance, were poured into toilet bowls in the forward heads, from which the oil trickled into the sea. "The effect of this film was almost instantaneous," said Dixon. "I watched huge greybeards,

Cozy sanctums for skippers and their mates

For all their glory of sail aloft, below-decks the windjammers were vast cargo bins with few comforts for the men beyond bare-planked tables and narrow bunks. But there was one grand exception to the spartan rule: the captain's sanctum, where the opulence could rival that of a mansion ashore.

On the American bark *Florence*, for example, the captain's quarters had red plush settees, a marble-topped table, a reed organ and a zinc-lined bathtub. The *Florence*'s owners thought nothing was too good for a man who had surmounted all the obstacles on the road to command. They expected him to live well, ashore and afloat.

In one fashion or another, as can be seen here, most shipowners subscribed to that idea. Indeed, so cozy were the quarters that many a captain brought his wife along—which had a wonderful way of ensuring he would take good care of ship and cargo.

Captain Harrison of the Eva Montgomery attends to some paper work while his wife reads.

The master of an unidentified windjammer sits at leisure with his lady in a suite containing a piano, beveled mirrors and a fur rug.

Aboard the Puritan, Captain and Mrs. Fred Amesbury had a windup victrola for their amusement in their lavishly furnished cabin.

A marble mantel, bouquets of flowers and a caged canary give Captain and Mrs. E. Gates James all the comforts of a Victorian parlor aboard the Lynton.

with ten-foot crests, come roaring up, only to be flattened down harmlessly as soon as they struck the oil."

But the *Arctic Stream* soon outran the slick, and the seas were now throwing the rudder clear out of the water—something that no oil could counter. Dixon ordered that heavy hauling lines be brought from the storage compartment, made fast to bitts and paid out over the stern. "Six hundred feet of them," said Dixon. "The drag was enormous, and it operated just at the moments when it was most needed—when the ship was balanced on the huge waves, with her rudder coming out of the water. The ship steered much better."

Next day the sky cleared and Dixon had a chance to take his position. The gods had smiled on him. Somehow the *Arctic Stream* had passed safely through the baleful channel between Cape Horn and the Diego Ramírez rocks and was now in the clear Atlantic.

During the *Arctic Stream*'s ordeal, the race with the *Herzogin Sophie Charlotte* had been forgotten, but now the mate glumly remarked that the contest was surely lost. No such thing, thought Dixon: "I knew there was still a chance to overhaul her, by putting my knowledge of meteorology to the test. I knew that the winds followed a certain sequence in these latitudes, and I calculated that if I kept on eastward, instead of turning north, as was the usual custom, I would fall in with more favorable winds that would carry me into the Trades. I therefore stood out across the Atlantic, hundreds of miles east of the ship lanes, and then turned north. My theory worked."

It did indeed. The *Arctic Stream* surged ahead for 4,800 miles under every bit of canvas she could carry, including the royals, without once changing a sail or hauling around a yard. At last, with C. C. Dixon gazing from her poop, the *Arctic Stream* entered the Strait of Dover—just three days behind the *Herzogin Sophie Charlotte*. Despite the fantastic odds against him, Dixon had exactly matched his rival in sailing time. He then raced on to Rotterdam, picking up still more time on the *Herzogin Sophie Charlotte* and arriving in Rotterdam the same day she reached Bremen. All told, the voyage had taken Dixon 97 days, and he could claim, if not actual victory, a moral triumph of epic proportions.

The great windjammer masters had in common at least one characteristic: they were all drivers, taking calculated risks, piling on sail whenever they could and shortening it with great reluctance, tacking rather than wearing their ships, and heaving to only as a last resort.

James Learmont, a six-foot Scotsman with a blunt tongue and a keen sense of honesty, was a legend in his own time for the speed and daring of his passages. Not that he was foolhardy; far from it. He knew the rulebook backward and forward, but he was so superb a mariner that he could afford to throw away the book when he wanted—which was often.

Learmont learned the fundamentals starting at age 12 on a coastal schooner owned by his father, a stern taskmaster, and by 15 he was ready for deep-sea ships. But though an apprentice-officer's berth was his for the asking, he resolved to begin as an ordinary seaman and "come 'through the hawse pipes' "—a decision not lightly taken. Young Lear-

Mustered on deck for an informal portrait after a lumbering six months at sea from Belfast to San Francisco, the crew of the British ship Rathdown lounges about the mizzenmast while their captain assumes a more studied stance at center foreground. A racially integrated crew like this one was not uncommon during the heyday of windjammers, when some of the best sailors were the black inhabitants of the West Indies and the Cape Verdes.

mont wanted to know and excel at every phase of sailing, and he felt that apprentices received inadequate training for command. Before he was 19 he had qualified for second mate's papers and was already becoming known as a cool, capable hand, the right man to have around in a crisis.

One night in 1896, on board the full-rigged ship *William Law* near Cape Horn, young Learmont notified his captain that he had sighted land looming on the port beam, and only a half hour away. The captain, whose navigating had evidently been faulty, loftily dismissed the suggestion—only to realize his error a few minutes later as he drove his ship in a stiff following wind ever closer to disaster. Aghast, he asked Learmont what to do. "Haul her to the wind," replied Learmont, "and sail her." The captain by now appeared paralyzed, so the young second mate took over the windjammer. He brought her around into the roaring wind, supervised the bracing of the yards, piled on more sail and all through the night conned the ship as close to the wind as he dared. By dawn the *William Law* was well away from the menacing shore and out of danger.

In 1902, when he was only 26, Learmont became a full-fledged windjammer captain and immediately set about getting faster passages out of his ships than anyone had previously. His first command, the 1,250-ton full-rigged *Brenhilda,* had been known as a bit of a dog, but in the South Atlantic on his very first passage Learmont drove her to a virtually unbeatable mark of 288 miles in 18 hours for an average speed of 16 knots. In the powerful northwesterly winds, said Learmont, "she was literally lifting out of the water under a heavy pressure of canvas."

Six years later, in another ship, the *Bengairn,* Learmont encountered a large field of icebergs east of the Horn—and characteristically decided to sail out of it at full speed, with every piece of canvas set. In the process he overtook a four-masted bark, the *Fingal* of Dublin, whose master had timidly shortened down to topsails. "We must have presented a wonderful sight to them," Learmont said later, "coming up from astern with royals set and doing 12 knots while they under topsails were doing about four." Observing nautical custom, Learmont hoisted his ship's ensign and his code number to identify himself. The *Fingal* did not deign to reply, and Learmont, miffed, airily signaled "Goodbye." And goodbye it was, for the *Bengairn* beat the *Fingal* to Hamburg by three weeks.

To such an exploit the Scottish owner of Learmont's ships, Captain John Rae of Liverpool, paid rare praise. "Learmont," he said, "you made a good passage. That was through havin' a good grip o' the watter."

Learmont was unshakable. Coming up the English Channel in the *Brenda* in 1905, he found himself confronted with changing weather conditions that called for repeated shifts in course—even while Learmont was also spending a good deal of time below looking after his pregnant wife, whose delivery time was near. Throughout a long night he supervised the handling of the ship personally or through his mates while he was tending his wife. In the morning he came on deck and saw that a severe squall was coming up. Instead of heaving to, he cracked on under nearly full sail, and the *Brenda* sped past Dover at 18 knots. When the squall cleared, she was through the Strait. "After setting the course," he later recalled, "I handed her over to the mate and went below. Three hours later the baby girl was born. All was well and I was grateful."

If Learmont was renowned for his speed, he was equally famed for his dustups with the vast, swarming bureaucracy of shore officials. For dealing with these parasites, Learmont had a simple rule: "Fight the shore bastards." In that spirit he caused dismay among harbor officials in Newcastle in 1908 when he arrived to take on a cargo of coal and ignored a standard port procedure. Since empty ships with their tall masts and heavy yards were vulnerable to capsizing, it was required that all ships be moved from the loading and unloading wharves to a special harbor area. There they would take on temporary stiffening ballast and then wait to return to the wharves. But Learmont had no intention of yielding his wharf position; it would mean missing his sailing date. He announced that he would take on no stiffening and would remain where he was until the coal could be loaded. And while horrified officials speculated as to his mental state, Learmont lowered all his royal and topgallant yards to the deck, thereby dropping the ship's center of gravity enough to make her stable. The method worked—but few other captains adopted it because, even with a full crew and experienced men, it was

Haunting tales spun by a master mariner

The square-riggers of the late 19th Century had their most eloquent interpreter in Joseph Conrad, whose haunting tales of the sea were woven from his own adventures as a sailor and master for nearly 20 years.

Conrad was born Jozef Teodor Konrad Korzeniowski, the scion of an aristocratic Polish family. But the appeal of the leisurely life quickly faded for the restless youth, and he left Cracow in 1874 at 17 to enlist as an apprentice seaman on a French West Indies trader. Within four years, he had decided to make a career at sea.

He won his mate's papers at 23 and his master's certificate *(below)* when he was 29. His first ship was a lovely little Australian bark called the *Otago;* "amongst her companions," Conrad wrote, "she looked like an Arab steed in a string of carthorses."

The thoroughbred *Otago* soon surpassed even Captain Conrad's expectations. On his first voyage she was caught in a hard gale on the passage from Singapore to Sydney. Under two lower topsails and a reefed foresail, the *Otago* raced at maximum speed for three days. The ship's performance was sheer poetry to Conrad, and he later described it in a memorable passage in *The Mirror of the Sea:*

"The solemn thundering combers caught her up from astern, passed her with a fierce boiling up of foam level with the bulwarks, swept on ahead with a swish and a roar: and the little vessel, dipping her jib-boom into the tumbling froth, would go on running in a smooth, glassy hollow, a deep valley between two ridges of the sea, hiding the horizon ahead and astern.

"There was such fascination in her pluck, nimbleness, the continual exhibition of unfailing seaworthiness, in the semblance of courage and endurance, that I could not give up the delight of watching her run."

For 14 months, Conrad, nicknamed "the Russian Count" by his crewmen, pushed the *Otago* before the wind, voyaging as far as Mauritius in the Indian Ocean. Off the north coast of Australia, Conrad executed a daring shortcut through the dangerous reef-strewn Torres Strait, fulfilling his boyhood dream "to haunt the scenes of the earthly exploits" of the great explorer, Captain James Cook.

Returning to England in 1889, Conrad embarked upon his life's work as a writer of fiction. Two years later, he signed on as the first mate of the *Torrens,* a famously swift British passenger clipper. Conrad made two voyages to Australia on the *Torrens,* but by 1894 he had parted from the sea forever, writing: "I had given myself up to the idleness of a haunted man who looks for nothing but words wherein to capture his visions."

Bearded Joseph Conrad, center, served as chief officer aboard the Torrens, making two runs from London to Adelaide, Australia, from 1891 to 1893.

The master's certificate obtained by Joseph Conrad at 29 qualified him for command.

thought too big a job to raise and lower the heavy, cumbersome yards.

It goes without saying that shipmasters did not enjoy being cheated in port, but after long and cheerless experience, many were resigned to it. Not James Learmont. Possessed of a mind that would have equipped him for a successful career in finance, he was quick to see through any attempts to bilk him, and obdurate enough to have his way. He once disputed a bill that had been rendered by a marine surveyor, tore it up in the man's face, called it a pack of lies and demanded a revised reckoning—which he got and paid. Again, while the ship was docked in a Chilean port, the crew complained to Learmont that the meat purchased there was inedible. When the butcher next showed up at the gangway, the captain was waiting for him. Ordering the man to empty his bag on the hatch, Learmont saw that the contents were mostly bones—and not very appetizing bones at that. He picked up the lot and threw it overboard. When the butcher protested, Learmont threw him after the meat.

In at least one instance, Learmont helped both ships and shipmasters on a grand scale. At the port of Callao, Peru, a local dock company, in league with a crooked harbor master, had for years short-weighted ships on the ballast required to take them safely to another port for their next cargo. With inadequate ballast, several vessels had disappeared; presumably they had capsized.

Learmont broke the murderous racket. First, he notified the harbor master that he wanted his ballast weighed as it went into the ship. It was a familiar demand to the harbor master, and he blandly ignored it. When part of the ballast had been delivered with its total weight merely estimated, Learmont refused to sign for it. At this the shifty harbor master said he lacked the necessary weighing equipment. Learmont countered by telling him how to devise a makeshift scale. The man reluctantly agreed, and a sample weighing was conducted in the presence of a dozen shipmasters. The test showed much less ballast than had been estimated—a fact that impressed the shipmasters but not the harbor master.

Loading continued until the dock company had provided what it claimed was adequate. Learmont refused to accept its figure and lodged a protest with the British Minister in Lima. Nothing came of it. The harbor master ordered Learmont to move his ship. The captain said he would not do so until he had received the 180 tons of ballast still due him. When the harbor master said he would have the ship moved, Learmont dared him to touch her. At that point the harbor master gave in. Stubborn James Learmont got his full load of ballast, the short-weighting ceased—and no more ships disappeared from Callao.

Captain Learmont was a surprising man, and in 1910 he sprang his greatest surprise: he announced his retirement from the deep-sea trades. He was scarcely 35. But he had been at sea since his boyhood, he had a family, and he had decided to become a pilot. His owner was dismayed and offered him a raise. His crewmen were desolate, and with good reason: in his years as a master, Learmont had lost only two men at sea—a pair of young Irishmen named Dunphy and Murphy who were pitched from an upper topsail in a stinking gale. But now, as always, Learmont was adamant. At the signing off of his last crew, an elderly Finnish carpenter who had served with him in all his ships presented himself to the collector of customs, who was in charge of the procedures, without his discharge book. When the collector expressed annoyance, the carpenter merely said, "I don't think that I will go back to sea again." He pointed to Learmont, who was standing nearby, and added: "If I should, it would be only with this man."

Another Scotsman, equally shrewd though of less lofty purpose and of more common clay than Learmont, was Captain W. S. "Old Jock" Leask of the *City of Florence*. As described by David W. Bone, then an apprentice under Leask and later a steamship commodore, Old Jock emerges as one of the more delightful characters in the authentic literature of the sea. He was an ungainly man, of medium height, stocky and rough-featured, with "keen grey eyes peering from beneath bushy eyebrows," and he gave his commands in a thick burr. While his ship was nearing San Francisco on a run from Glasgow, a slow, smouldering fire broke out in a cargo of coal in the forward hold, badly blistering the hull paint on the starboard bow. Old Jock instantly realized that the fire must be hidden from the tugboat captain bringing the ship through the Golden Gate; if he knew, he could demand a heavy salvage fee rather than a modest towing toll, and that, to Old Jock, would have been unthinkable.

Seeking to conceal the evidence of the blaze, Leask maneuvered the bark so that the tug captain would have to approach it from the port side. Meanwhile, just in case, he ordered his mate to keep the hot patch freshly painted. To open the bargaining, the tug captain asked $600 as a towing fee. Old Jock scoffed at the figure. "Holy smoke! I don't want t'buy yer boat, Capt'in," he called, and with a fine show of seriousness ordered his mate to set sail preparatory to coming into the harbor unassisted. "Loose them royals, Mister! Six hundred, no damn fear!" The tug veered off, by happy chance staying to port, then returned. This time her captain offered a slightly lower fee, which was also rejected out of hand.

By now, the newly applied paint having blistered, another coat had been surreptitiously slapped on. Eventually a second tugboat heaved into sight, and the first tug's captain, fearful of losing the job entirely, offered his tow for $300, to which Old Jock made a grand display of reluctant acceptance. Finally at Benita Point, Leask ran up signal flags informing the ship's agents ashore that the *Florence* was afire, and only when the fire barge came did the tug captain realize he had been taken.

With the fire doused and the remaining coal unloaded, the *Florence* took on grain and headed back around the Horn for Falmouth. Off the Cape she encountered violent weather, with following seas threatening repeatedly to engulf her; Old Jock stood by the helmsman through an entire night and day, steadily conning the ship and giving calm commands. "Unkempt and haggard, blue-lipped, drenched by sea and rain," recalled Bone, "he was never less than a Master of the Sea." A day or two later, east of the Horn, the wind abated and Old Jock went below for some desperately needed rest. But soon fog enveloped the ship. All was still. The lookout was ordered to sound the foghorn.

He blew three blasts. R-R-R-R-R-AH! R-R-R-R-R-AH! R-R-R-R-R-AH!

Suddenly the men on watch looked at each other. Had they heard an answering blast? The foghorn was sounded again and, sure enough, they heard three faint responses. Was there another ship nearby? The mate decided to call the captain. Arriving on the poop, Old Jock ordered the foghorn sounded again, and listened carefully. No sooner had the first answering note come back than he moved into thunderous action.

"Down hellum! DOWN HELLUM! DOWN," he yelled, running aft to the wheel. "Haul yards! Le'go port braces! Let 'm rip! Quick, Mist'r! Christ! What ye standin' at?. Ice! Ice, ye bluidy eedi't! Ice! Th' echo! LE'GO AN' HAUL! LE'GO!"

The *Florence* came alive as yards swung, blocks whirred, sails lifted and men hurried to bring her about. She responded, coming up toward the wind, as the captain stood by the compass, sniffing, looking into the fog. Nothing. Silence.

Then the sky brightened, the fog lifted a bit, and there it was. A solid wall of ice, with the bark drifting toward it. Just then the bow lookout shouted, "Stop!" In front of him the crew could see a small calf berg, a couple of dozen feet high, near the bows. In seconds the *Florence* struck it. The bowsprit broke with a loud snap, and down came the fore-topgallant mast with all its yards and sails, hurtling to the deck and punching a hole in it. The sound of grinding, splintering and hammering was deafening. A huge chunk of ice crashed onto the forehatch, shattering it. All hands prepared to abandon ship.

As Old Jock had foreseen the calamity, now he suddenly sensed a way out. Amid all the confusion, he had noticed that the wind had shifted

Caught by a sudden gust of wind without sufficient ballast in her hold to steady her, the recently fitted-out windjammer Jacques lies helplessly on her beam-ends in the Tancarville Canal near Le Havre, France, in 1900. The accident, though uncommon, was an expensive one when it happened; in this case all three of the Jacques's masts had to be cut away before the 1,900-ton vessel could be righted.

just a touch, making it possible for the *Florence* to sail clear. "Fore-yards!" yelled the captain. "Le' go an' haul!" The *Florence* came round farther and gathered headway. As she did, the broken jib boom began slamming against the bows. "Cut and clear away!" roared Old Jock. "Let her go!" The boom dropped into the sea—and the crippled bark headed for the open ocean.

Old Jock and his crew made their own repairs in the Falkland Islands, and the *Florence* set out in good trim for Falmouth. Yet one last trial was in store for the bark and her master before the voyage was over. At Falmouth the *Florence* was directed to proceed to Sligo, on the north-west coast of Ireland, to deliver her grain. She would be guided by a Welsh coasting pilot, a voluble sort whom Leask regarded with deep and abiding distrust. Late one afternoon the pilot announced that the rocky outcropping to the lee was the Stags—Sligo should not be far off. "Indeed to goodness," he said with pompous assurance (as Bone tells the story), "it iss the best landfall I haf ever seen, Capt'in!" The weather was poor and a gray mist hung over the coastline. Leask consulted his charts and gazed at the rocks: his book of sailing directions said there were four Stags. "Damme!" he muttered, "I can only see three."

"D'ye know the Stags well, Mister?" he quizzed the pilot. "Are ye sure o' ye're ground?"

"Well, well!" the pilot laughed. "I know the Stags, yess! Ass well ass I know Car-narvon!" said the pilot, referring to the Welsh port. "East south-east now, Capt'in, an' a fine run to Sligo Bar!"

Leask was unconvinced. Night, black and moonless, came as Old Jock paced the poop deck. Then came the desperate scream of the lookout through the dark: "Brea—kers a-head!"

As if he had expected and prepared for the worst, the captain turned calmly to the helmsman. "Luff! Down helm, an' keep her close!" If he could bring the bark about, she might clear the rocks. Even in the instant of crisis, he paused to express contempt for the pilot. "Hoo many Stags d'ye know, Mister? T'hell wi' you an' yer bloody Stags." And to the mate, "All hands, there, Mister. Up, ye hounds; up, if ye look fur dry buryin'!"

Terrified, the crew piled on sail. The bark picked up speed, began turning and heeled way over, her lee rail coursing through the water. The wind had become almost a gale. Leask stood at the gangway, talking to the ship. "Stand, good spars." He patted the taffrail. "Up tae it, ye bitch! Up!! Into it! T'wind'ard!" Yards and masts seemed to bend under the strain, but they held firm. The bark drew nearer the rocks. Then with agonizing slowness she began to come around. The second mate report-ed that the compass was swinging—half a point, anyway. The wind screamed in the rigging. To the helmsman, Old Jock admonished, "Full, m' lad! Keep 'er full. Goad, man! Steer as ye never steered." The ship staggered on, turning ever so slowly.

"Nae higher! Nae higher!" shouted Leask, fearing that she would be taken aback by pointing directly into the wind. "Dinna let her gripe." Suddenly a narrow stretch of clear water appeared between her bow and the reef. She rushed along it—to safety. The ship came out into the open water, and Old Jock clapped his hand to his head. "Done it, ye bitch! Done it! Weathered—by Goad!"

In all-around technical proficiency, the crack German captains were without peer. And the master who set standards of excellence that lasted long after he had left the sea was Robert Hilgendorf, tall, hawk-nosed, with eyes as blue and as icy as the Baltic from whose shores he came.

Hilgendorf was an enigma. His was a name to be murmured in awe— or muttered in envy—in harbor taverns from Hamburg to Iquique. He spoke in aphorisms: his motto was, "The best of speed in the interests of the firm"; his policy toward crewmen was, "Hard work, but good food"; his dictum on manners and morals was, "One can never drink too little— but easily too much!"

Myths, many of them preposterous and masking the true nature of his genius, were spun around him. He would, it was said, let his canvas be blown away rather than take in sail; lest fearful sailors try to take that decision into their own hands, the stories went, he padlocked his sheets, and himself stood guard at the halyards with a revolver. In fact, records show no excessive sail damage on Hilgendorf ships, and it was impossible to padlock the sails.

He was called "the Devil of Hamburg" by jealous men of lesser talent, who argued that his skill with the wind could come only from an unholy partnership. Even those most admiring of Hilgendorf hinted at a touch of the mystical. Once, when he had closeted himself to examine his charts, someone remarked softly: "The Old One is doing his magic again." Said a fellow captain: "The trouble with him was that he was somehow different from the rest of us. He really did have that extraordinary sixth sense for the wind. Even the wind seemed to know that."

Yet what some men took to be unearthly was in fact the result of Hilgendorf's rare application to the seaman's profession. "Hilgendorf," wrote Alan Villiers, "was a scientist—a sailing scientist."

He was born in 1852 in a small town on Stettin Lagoon on the Baltic. When his father, a captain of a small peat boat sailing out of Stettin, went into the army to fight as a foot soldier against Denmark in 1864, young Robert, only 12, took over his father's little vessel. At 17, he was an able seaman working the Baltic and the North Sea. It was a harsh, cold trade—small, leaky ships performing drudge chores in the worst of weather—and by the time that Hilgendorf had earned his master's papers and, at the age of 27, presented his certificate at the Hamburg shipping firm of Reederei F. Laeisz, he was a harsh, cold man. "Captain Hilgendorf was a very hard master to please," said a former crewman, "but he was a splendid captain and navigator."

The Germans approached navigation with Teutonic thoroughness. In Hamburg's Hydrographic Office a staff of four labored over one of the world's first systematic studies of the oceans in all their moods. Shipmasters were required to report, for example, on the latitude and longitude at which they met the trade winds, on vagaries encountered in the doldrums and the horse latitudes, on winds here and currents there in all seasons—and, always, on the details of beating around the Horn. Some masters might ignore or scoff at the Hydrographic Office reports. Not Hilgendorf. He devoured them, remembered them—and put them to use. Therein lay the secret considered by so many to be beyond mortal ken.

Hilgendorf was a private person, little given to self-glorification, and

Salty ritual at the equator

King Neptune, with his queen and motley retinue, holds court at the equator in 1912 aboard the German windjammer Elfrieda.

While a hitch before the mast on a windjammer meant mostly hard work and flinty hardtack, there was one time when a seaman could expect a bit of levity and a tot or two of rum.

Tradition required that whenever a ship crossed the equator—and windjammers, because of the nature of their trade, almost invariably did so on each voyage—all on board who had never crossed the line must submit to a rite of passage that transformed them from green hands to full-fledged shellbacks. And for a brief spell, the ship sailed under the anarchic flag of King Neptune, who decreed unbridled revelry.

As the ship approached the equator, a hoarse voice would command that the vessel heave to, and the seaman playing Neptune would climb over the bows, dripping sea water and swearing amid a cacophony of whistles, combs, saucepan lids and coffeepots. Accompanying him was a rogues' gallery of attendants—his queen, Amphitrite, made up as a whore; a judge, carrying a roll of those to be baptized; a priest; a doctor; a barber and guards with painted faces.

After an interlude for refreshments, Neptune summoned the unfortunates to trial. A rigorous interrogation followed, dwelling on the green hands' ancestry and manhood, after which they were all found to be a landlubberly lot, unclean and in dire need of a shave and bath.

Often the barbering began the instant a postulant opened his mouth to reply to a question and got a brush— usually lathered with coal tar and soap —thrust into it. He was then scraped from chin to crown with a razor made from a barrel hoop.

Next the wretched green hand was toppled into a tub of sea water (often blindfolded so he might think himself overboard) and mercilessly scrubbed by Neptune's guards, chanting:

Shave him and bash him,
Duck him and splash him,
Torture and smash him,
And don't let him go.

The victim was then made to swear that he would always impose the same ritual on future green hands, whereupon he was accorded a certificate of baptism to the rank of a well- and truly hardened shellback.

contemporary accounts offer only fleeting glimpses of the man in action—always cool, always calculating. One of his finest hours came during what must have seemed to him the nadir of his career. He and the lovely bark *Parsifal,* bound for Chile with 1,500 tons of coal aboard, were about 25 miles south of Cape Horn when heavy weather struck. With a roar, the entire cargo shifted to one side of the hold. Hilgendorf instantly ordered that the masts be chopped down, an action that, though it prevented the *Parsifal* from capsizing, left her helpless before the heaving seas. The *Parsifal*'s bottom sprang leaks and, even as the water began to rise in her hold, a strange sail was sighted in the distance. Hilgendorf showed a distress signal. Then he and his men took to the boats and began pulling toward the other ship—which continued, unknowing, on its way and disappeared from view.

It was then that Hilgendorf really rose to the occasion: instead of rowing toward land, he calmly ordered the boats back to the rapidly sinking *Parsifal.* To have any hope of survival at sea, or on the desolate Horn for that matter, they would need provisions: food, water, blankets. Hilgendorf and his men courageously clambered back on board the foundering, listing craft and fought their way below to the storage casks and lockers. The *Parsifal* might go down at any minute. With the sweat of anxiety bathing their brows, the men swiftly collected what they could and hastened back topside. They had just cleared the *Parsifal* and were rowing away when the stricken windjammer went down in the vortex of her own whirlpool.

As it turned out, the supplies were not needed. By great good fortune, the British bark *Saraka* spotted a flare from the boats that night and picked up Hilgendorf and his men. All hands had survived the disaster.

During 20 years Hilgendorf commanded nine windjammers for the Laeisz firm. He rounded the Horn no fewer than 66 times and, in so doing, set marks for speed and consistency that freight steamers would not equal for another quarter century. Before Hilgendorf, any passage to a Chilean port in less than 80 days was considered good, and shipmasters always counted on from two to three weeks for rounding the Horn. Hilgendorf's average outward passage was 64 days, his return 74 days, and his average speed, with deep-loaded vessels in storm and in calm, was seven and a half knots. He made it around the Horn in as few as seven days and on no passage did he take more than 10 days. His record, as amazing now as then, was written in his logs: "*Pirat*—Channel to Valparaiso, 68 days. *Pergamon*—Channel to Valparaiso, 65 days. *Palmyra*—Channel to Valparaiso, 63 days. *Placilla*—Channel to Valparaiso, 58 days. *Potosi*—off-Channel to Valparaiso, 55 days."

In 1901, at age 49 and without a word of explanation, Robert Hilgendorf stopped doing his magic. He retired as a master and spent his next 30 years as a marine surveyor and an appraiser for marine insurance companies. In February 1937, in his eighties, he died after a bicycle accident in Hamburg. He was, after all, mortal.

Robert Miethe, one of Hilgendorf's fellow Laeisz captains, held his ships in respect and affection. "To us," he once said, "the ship was a sort of living thing, and master and crew were with her to serve her."

Blessed with an uncanny sense for wind and ocean currents that earned him a reputation as a navigational wizard, Robert Hilgendorf became the stuff of legend during his 20 years as a windjammer skipper for the Laeisz shipping concern of Hamburg. Among his numerous accomplishments was the remarkable feat of making two round trips in less than one year between Hamburg and the nitrate fields along Chile's northwest coast.

Miethe was close to the sea and to ships all his life. Born in a small Holstein village within sight of the Baltic, he shipped out at 14 on a small vessel engaged in dredging up stones from the seabed for use in building the Kiel Canal. Two years later he became a deck boy on a Laeisz bark, rising on steadily through the ranks to command five company ships.

A solidly built, determined man with penetrating gray-blue eyes and an enormous voice, Miethe was imperturbable in the face of danger or pain. Once, while he was standing on the midship deck of a Laeisz bark, a massive sea slammed him against some heavy metal rigging. His collarbone was broken, one of his kneecaps was dislocated and a big gash in his head gushed blood. Helped up by the mate, Miethe first determined that the ship was all right and then allowed himself to be carried below, where he took charge of his own treatment. He supervised the strapping of his shoulder, told the mate to knock his kneecap back with a belaying pin and then directed him to sew up his scalp: "Pinch the sides together and sew like a sailmaker!" After 24 stitches, the captain returned to work.

His true beloved was Laeisz's *Pitlochry*, a beautiful Scottish-built four-masted bark that he commanded between 1908 and 1911. The *Pitlochry* was one of those blessed craft in which all the key design elements—hull configuration, deck arrangement, sail plan and rigging—somehow combine to produce a perfect sailing ship. All her masters were fond of her, and none more than Miethe. As he put it, "She listened to the wind better than any ship I ever had."

The *Pitlochry* was so responsive to the helm that Miethe could have been forgiven for hoping that someday he would be given an opportunity to demonstrate her glory to an appreciative audience. He got that chance one sweet summer day when the *Pitlochry* was beating up the English Channel. By chance, she happened to be standing in toward Brighton at a time when visitors crowded the resort. Bands were playing, the air was festive and the famous pier was jammed. All at once the vacationers became aware that a big square-rigged ship was sailing toward them, drawing closer and closer. All of the windjammer's sails were set, their white shapes billowing magnificently toward the sky.

On and on she came, silently, the foam curling from her bows. Then, when the *Pitlochry* was hardly more than a few ships' lengths from the end of the pier, Robert Miethe began to put her about. As he gave the commands, the helm was thrust over, lower sails were swiftly clewed up, the spanker brought around, jib sheets let go and yards braced to a new tack. The crowd could hear the orders being shouted and could see sailors racing along the decks, hauling at the lines and sheets. As the mammoth vessel turned, now only a hundred yards or so from the throng, she slowed down, her sails flapping and yards still swinging, then caught the wind from the new beam and began to pick up headway again. As she pulled away, her sails filled once more with wind, the crowd cheered. Years later Miethe, still affected by the memory, said, "A man may know an occasion like that only once in a lifetime."

But there were many other memorable occasions for Miethe to look back on in old age. And on one of them Miethe demonstrated the supreme quality that no book and no mentor could teach. All the great

captains were born with it and refined it with experience into the clear, pure essence of seafaring. It was that instinct for the right move at the right time that unfailingly enabled them to surmount the perils that would crush lesser men.

The date was 1909, and the ship had been moving smartly through the English Channel under brisk winds, sometimes making 16 knots. But off the Dutch coast the wind died and she was becalmed. The barometer dropped, then held steady. In the ominous stillness Miethe noticed there were no sea birds around—a sure sign of impending foul weather.

There were fitful whispers of wind for several hours, then a breeze came up, first from the south. Then it shifted more strongly from the northwest. The *Pitlochry* began to move and picked up good speed. As the short December day came to an end and darkness set in, Miethe shortened his vessel down to topsails, foresail and her strongest staysails, good running gear for a storm. The tempest struck: a furious squall of hail pounded against the sails and rattled on the deck.

The *Pitlochry* was almost at the mouth of the Elbe, the point at which she would customarily pick up her pilot. But no pilot boat appeared. Because the wind was too strong to permit tacking and there was not

Robert Miethe (right), the last of a series of legendary German windjammer captains who battled Cape Horn for the Flying P Line, is shown in an old photograph entertaining agents and fellow skippers in the genial glow of the master's cabin aboard his ship, the Pitlochry, at anchor in Tocopilla, Chile. Miethe was single-mindedly dedicated to the big square-riggers. Years later, after they had vanished from the seas, he remarked, "I did not leave sailing ships. They left me."

enough room to wear ship, it was now too late to turn back toward the open sea; Miethe, on his own, would have to make a run for an anchorage far enough upriver to escape the storm's full fury.

The captain knew that the river mouth was marked by five lightships, numbered 1 to 5, leading toward Hamburg. He also knew that he might find a good holding ground for his anchors near a sandbank called the Mittelrüg, not far from the fifth lightship. All the *Pitlochry*'s hands were at their stations: Miethe conning the ship from the compass platform near the poop, crewmen standing by the various winches and braces, and the first mate, aided by the carpenter, sailmaker and blacksmith, ready on the forecastlehead to cut the anchors loose and operate the windlass. The anchors had been put in a preparatory position on the davit-like catheads at the bow; a sharp, hard blow at their retaining pins with a heavy maul would send both of them plunging into the water.

Visibility was bad, although some river lights could now be made out. Soon the *Pitlochry* came up on the first lightship, Elbe 1, and flew past it. There seemed no way of slowing her. The main lower topsail blew out and disappeared into the night. The *Pitlochry*'s speed did not slacken. Elbe 2 and 3 were passed even as the storm increased in intensity, and Miethe felt his face stung not only by hail but by flying sand, a sure sign of some nearby shoal or sandbank. He was certain the ship, aided by a flood tide, was making at least 18 knots.

When Elbe 4 came into sight and disappeared astern, it was imperative that Miethe slow down. He took in the fore lower topsail; crewmen climbed aloft and out along the icy footropes to make the sail snug to the yard. The *Pitlochry* slowed measurably, and Elbe 5 appeared ahead. So, however, did a maze of lights. The anchorage area seemed alive with vessels, most of them large steamships, that had sought safety near the Mittelrüg. Miethe peered into the light and tried to pick a spot. The last lightship, Elbe 5, was abeam and the critical moment was at hand. Miethe shouted to the helmsman: "Hard a-starboard!" The wheel was spun, and the *Pitlochry* faithfully responded, turning in what seemed an instant and coming right up into the wind. "Let go anchors!" The mate and the sailmaker swung their mauls and sent the anchors splashing down, first one and then the other. Behind them came the anchor cable, pounding out through the hawsepipes. It stopped. The cables stretched taut—and held firm. The *Pitlochry* was in.

Throughout the night the crew stood by, taking in the last sails. Miethe had soundings taken and found there was only a fathom of water under his keel. In the morning, to everyone's surprise, the buoy marking the Mittelrüg sandbar was only 50 yards astern, and all about the *Pitlochry* steamers were riding out the storm, some with their propellers turning to keep them in place. The *Pitlochry* seemed to have found—her captain had found—the only available spot in the anchorage.

It was not until a day later that a pilot could get out to the windjammer. "Good God, Captain, how did you get here? Where did you come from?" "From Tocopilla," replied Robert Miethe. "Sixty-three days."

Characteristically, he gave the *Pitlochry* all the credit for the incredible anchorage. "She found it," said Miethe, "I only recognized it. So there she was, my good and faithful ship, come safely in from sea."

Recollections of youthful fo'c's'le adventure

Evidently amused by his own work, marine artist Anton Otto Fischer sits before a painting that depicts an angry seaman discovering that his pockets have been rifled.

An orphan who was utterly miserable as the ward of an unloving uncle in Regensburg, Bavaria, Anton Otto Fischer was 15 and working as a printer's apprentice in 1898 when a poster in the window of a travel agency caught his eye. "The poster showed a sailing ship scudding along under full sail," he later wrote, "with wind-driven clouds revealing a blue sky over an ultramarine sea." Enchanted by this alluring scene, Fischer persuaded his uncle to allow him to go to sea. For the next five years, like thousands of lads in the last great age of sail, he experienced life in the fo'c's'le, with all its harshness and discomfort, its dangers and tragedies, as well as its comradeship and simple pleasures.

For three years Fischer served on Baltic traders. Then he signed on a deepwater windjammer, the *Gwydyr Castle*, a British bark headed around Cape Horn for Panama. "Here finally was the ship of my earlier dreams, and I walked up the gangplank and forward to the focs'le with a light step." Tossing his bag onto a bunk, Fischer settled into the cramped cabin behind the foremast that he would share for two years with 14 other sailors.

Outward-bound, the ship wallowed in the doldrums while tempers grew short and fights broke out. Predictably, Cape Horn greeted the ship with murderous weather. "Two months of purgatory in a watery hell," Fischer called it, adding that the rations became almost inedible. "We would pound the hardtack into pieces and drop them into our pannikins of hot tea or coffee. In a minute or so the weevils would rise to the surface to be skimmed off."

As the months wore on, Fischer became an able seaman. In 1903 the ship docked in New York and he was paid off, ending his windjammer days. He decided on a career as an artist, and in time became a well-known illustrator, appearing in the *Saturday Evening Post* and other publications. But of all his work, none evoked a greater sense of the adventure aboard a windjammer than a volume of paintings entitled *Focs'le Days* published in 1947. Several of these are reproduced here, accompanied by Fischer's comments.

Suspended in a bosun's chair beneath
the bowsprit of the Gwydyr Castle, Fischer
in this self-portrayal from his youth
adds a mischievous touch to the figurehead
while his ship languishes in the mid-
Atlantic doldrums in 1901. The artist later
recalled that he had "beautified the
regal lady with carmine lips and cheeks"
—an embellishment that made her
naughtily suggestive of a streetwalker.

Fighting his way aft with the officers'
food, the ship's steward braves green water
during a roaring gale. Detested for
having provisioned the ship with rancid
salt pork and weevil-ridden hardtack,
he received no sympathy from the crew
when he risked his life on deck. "The
sight of him," Fischer wrote, "clutching the
lifeline under his arm while holding
onto a dishpan in one hand and a coffee pot
in the other, trying to keep his footing,
always filled us with unholy glee."

Enraged after receiving inedible meat, the crew complains bitterly to the captain, who finally leans over for a judicious whiff while shipmates look on. The meat, wrote the artist, "looked exactly like a colored chunk of wood and was of about the same consistency. To prove our point, I produced the ship's model I had whittled from the first piece."

*Off duty in the forecastle, crewmen look
on with fascination as the ship's resident
artist, Fischer, tattoos a shipmate with
India ink. "We had no needle, but I found a
sharp steel pen and one dog-watch
I started in tattooing a full rigged ship
on Fatty Ecklund's chest. My prize
effort, though, was when I tattooed a naked
houri onto a fellow's bicep, so that
when he flexed his muscles, she did a sort
of hootchie-kootchie dance."*

Three seamen perform for their shipmates as the Gwydyr Castle lies off Panama in 1901, unloading coal. Unwilling to pay for local laborers, the parsimonious captain had the crew work 12 hours at a stretch in the hold, where "every pound of coal had to be discharged by hand," Fischer wrote. Small wonder that even the simple fo'c's'le music became a welcome "break in the numbing monotony of our existence."

"I tore into Tim with both arms flailing. Suddenly, after a wild mix-up, Tim was down on deck." So wrote Fischer of this fight between himself and a chronically truculent sailor who kept insulting Fischer until the two came to blows. A few days later Fischer's foe fell to his death from a yardarm. "I felt worse than anyone on board," wrote Fischer. "I would have given anything if Tim and I hadn't fought that bloody battle."

The Gwydr Castle's old sailmaker,
killed one night on deck when he stumbled
and hit his head on an iron ringbolt, is
buried at sea by his shipmates as the
captain intones a brief eulogy. "He was
a Swede and had served in the United
States Navy during the Civil War," wrote
Fischer sadly. "He was as grand an
old seadog as ever sailed the seven seas."

Chapter 3

A heyday of proud ships and hellships

Commerce thrives against a desolate backdrop as windjammers crowd the harbor of Iquique, about 1900, loading up with valuable Chilean nitrate.

n October 28, 1905, the windjammer *British Isles*, a three-masted full-rigged ship that had just completed a 139-day passage from Wales, dropped anchor three miles off the dust-caked port of Pisagua, on the west coast of Chile, and hoisted a flag signaling for a pilot. Aboard the *British Isles*, watching with fresh eyes and eager attention, was 15-year-old apprentice William H. Jones, who had just experienced the initial 10,000-mile leg of his first voyage. He was not to see home port—or his family—again until he had sailed more than 50,000 miles, crossed the Pacific four times and grown so tall his parents hardly recognized him. Now, from the deck of the *British Isles*, he could see yellow mud huts rimming the crescent-shaped shore of the bay; behind them and beyond an unseen tract of copper mines and nitrate deposits, the early-morning sun cast golden rays on the snow-capped peaks of the Andes, which rose, stark and treeless, into an azure sky. Between that spectacular backdrop and the *British Isles* rode some 20 sailing ships, swaying lazily in the rolling Pacific waters about half a mile offshore.

Before long, a pilot boat answered the *British Isle*'s signal and put out from shore. Then, Jones noted with astonishment, "from about ten of the anchored ships, boats also put out, and were rowed rapidly towards us in a race, their oars flashing in the sunlight as the crews of apprentices strove to be the first to reach us."

A ship's captain sat with lordly aplomb in the stern of each boat, urging on his oarsmen. Reaching the *British Isles*, "the captains came aboard, to greet our Old Man like a long-lost brother, and drink the last of his whisky, if he had any left, while also proffering advice, which was not heeded." But what Jones found most remarkable of all on that memorable day "was the sight of 30 skilled boys swarming on board to augment our sparse crew." The boys—the apprentices who had rowed their captains out—all set to work aboard the *British Isles*, amiably clewing and stowing sail, and generally assisting in the work of bringing the new arrival safely to her berth.

The profusion of vessels that William Jones encountered on the west coast of South America was nothing unusual, for he made his first voyage in the heyday of the windjammer. If a score of windjammers rode companionably at anchor off the remote and diminutive village of Pisagua, hundreds more were at ports up and down the coast—Tocopilla, Antofagasta and Iquique in Chile; Pisco, Callao and Lomas in Peru; Manta and Guayaquil in Ecuador. On the North American west coast, the harbors of San Francisco and Vancouver were a forest of masts, and hundreds upon hundreds of windjammers thronged other ports all over the world: Hamburg, London, Liverpool, Cardiff, Antwerp, Bordeaux, Dunkirk, Hong Kong, Shanghai, Rio de Janeiro, New York, Norfolk, Boston, Melbourne. In 1905, the year that William Jones made his first voyage, steel- and iron-hulled windjammers flew flags representing Great Britain, the United States, Italy, Belgium, France, Germany and the Scandinavian countries—nearly every seafaring nation of the world. More than 3,500 sailing ships were registered with the insurance firm of Lloyd's of London alone.

Counting officers, seamen and apprentices, some 150,000 mariners sailed the windjammers. And with all the shipwrights, stevedores, agents, managers and others on the shoreside establishment, something like 500,000 people were involved with these great tall ships. Some of the vessels belonged to financially sound, efficient and competitive companies headquartered in the great port cities, whence the ships sailed with prearranged contracts for delivering one cargo and immediately fetching another. Other vessels, operated by less effective companies or by individual owners, tramped from port to port on a catch-as-catch-can basis, picking up whatever cargo was available. Merchant, captain, apprentice and seaman—all served an industry that in 1898 was more than a $25 million business. As such, it was also a business that was competitive, cooperative, profitable, risky, lonely, romantic, harsh—and irresistible.

Although the Americans and the British had dominated sail through most of the 1800s, toward the end of the century they were overtaken by other nations. The United States, after its triumphant experience with clipper ships, was now exploiting its new transcontinental railway, developing the vast reaches of its interior and paying less attention to the sea. On the other side of the Atlantic, British shipowners were concentrating on steam; most of the square-riggers turned out by Britain's superb shipyards were sold abroad, principally to buyers in France, Germany, Italy and the Scandinavian nations. It was for the most part in these nations that dozens upon dozens of companies brought windjammers to their days of glory.

Of them all, two stood out: the German firm of Reederei F. Laeisz, for which the great captains Hilgendorf and Miethe sailed, and the French company of Antoine-Dominique Bordes et Fils. It was not so much size that made them conspicuous. About 200 ships sailed under the French tricolor in 1900, but only some 40 of them belonged to Bordes; the Laeisz fleet was smaller still, with rarely more than 16 ships. But though never the biggest, both companies distinguished themselves— the Germans for the wonderful efficiency of their operations afloat and ashore, the French for their Gallic *élan* and for ships that were as beautiful as they were swift and seaworthy. And both Laeisz and Bordes won fame and fortune for their shrewd and timely attention to the lucrative Chilean nitrate trade.

Nitrate was among the nastiest cargoes known to man—noxious, flammable and, when powdered and packed in bags for shipment, punishingly heavy. But between the years 1890 and 1914, it was also among the most profitable; the farmers of Europe were using 500,000 tons of it annually for fertilizer, and saber-rattling government leaders were demanding thousands of tons more for munitions. Europe had little sodium nitrate in its own soil. The only major source was thousands of sea miles away, in the deserts of Chile, a land so barren that even normally hardy mules dropped dead for want of pasturage and water as, laden with bags of nitrate, they made the 50-mile downhill trek from the mines to the waiting ships.

The coast was as inhospitable as the inland hills. It was subject to earthquakes and to occasional tidal waves. More common and quite as menacing were the northers—the sudden, violent storms that descended with gusts of wind up to 95 miles an hour; they could snap a ship's moorings or topple a poorly ballasted craft and turn a crowded anchorage into a confusion of damaged vessels come adrift. All this was in addition to the terrible perils of the roaring forties and Cape Horn that had to be conquered just to get there and back.

It required stout ships, skillfully manned, to withstand such challenges, and tight organization to capitalize on the dismal market. From their far-flung lairs in Hamburg and Paris, the firms of Laeisz and Bordes commanded both.

The Laeisz firm was founded in 1825 by patriarch Ferdinand B. Laeisz, a canny entrepreneur who got his start selling silk hats in Hamburg and soon found a market in South America, to which Germans were eventually to emigrate in growing numbers. Later he expanded into other merchandise. The company was doing a general export business in 1852, when Ferdinand's 24-year-old son, Carl Heinrich, joined his father—and soon thereafter the company was launched on a new venture, dispatching its merchandise around the world in its own ships. Ferdinand and Carl began their new undertaking modestly, with the purchase of a 22-year-old wooden schooner named *Sophie & Friedericke* in 1856. But in the same year, they took a more fateful step, ordering the building of a new 140-foot bark to their own specifications. They decided to name her in honor of Carl's young wife, Sophie.

Daughter of a well-to-do Hamburg ship broker, Sophie was nicknamed "Poodle" because of her luxuriant, curly hair. In affectionate jest, father and son called their new vessel *Pudel* and, by accident or by design, that was the start of a family variation on a seagoing convention that had begun with the clipper ships, whose owners ofttimes gave them names that linked them to their sister ships. Sir William Garthwaite, who owned the British company Marine Navigation, called his ships by names that bore the same first syllable as his own—such as *Garthforce*, *Garthgarry*, *Garthneill*, *Garthsnaid*, *Garthwray*. The Alaska Packers' Association *(page 149)* called its ships "stars": *Star of Bengal*, *Star of India*, *Star of Greenland*, *Star of Italy*. For the Laeisz family, ever after the launching of the *Pudel*, the distinguishing feature was to be the initial "P." When the firm purchased a bark called the *Flottbek*, she was renamed the *Professor*; another, named the *Aminta*, became the *Pluto*. In due course Laeisz ships became known as P liners, and as the firm acquired a reputation for speed, it came to be informally called the Flying P Line.

Within a decade the Laeisz fleet had grown to six ships, and by 1870 to 16. From then on, though the fleet did not change significantly in numbers, the gross tonnage increased spectacularly. The 16 ships of the 1870 fleet had a combined tonnage of 6,700. Two decades later the number of ships had dropped to 15—while the tonnage leaped to 18,245. Thereafter the tonnage continued to go up, to 30,229 in 1900 and to 39,485 in 1910. The major reason for the growth in tonnage, of course, was the advent of the huge steel windjammers starting in the mid-1880s.

The ships were not only large, they were also the best that modern

The benign gaze of Ferdinand B. Laeisz belies the shrewd financial judgment that he exercised as founder of the Hamburg shipping concern that for four generations carried his name on windjammers sailing around the world. By the 1880s the Flying P liners had made him a very rich man. He shared his good fortune with Hamburg, building rent-free apartments for the poor and an opera house for the rich.

Flying the ensign of the city of Hamburg from her spanker gaff, the bark Pudel—one of Ferdinand Laeisz's Flying P liners—rides in the city's floating dry dock on the Elbe River in this 1858 German painting. The dry dock, a cradle-like platform that could lift a vessel above the water line, was a Hamburg innovation; by making it no longer necessary to careen a ship and clean her hull one side at a time, the dry dock halved the time a ship had to spend in port.

ingenuity and efficiency could make them. They carried improved cargo winches and more powerful steam donkey engines that eliminated some of the backbreaking labor of bringing cargo aboard.

To good ships the Laeiszes added good men. Carl's instructions to his captains, carefully written out in longhand in 1892, began with a forthright statement in which there was an implicit command: "My vessels can and shall make fast passages." Together with orders for scrupulous maintenance of his ships, he wrote: "Next to skill in navigation, I value thrift." No waste was permitted; sails, masts, spars, rigging and anything else that was damaged on return to Hamburg had to be mended if at all possible. And what did need replacing had to be bought from trusty German manufacturers at home, where thrifty Laeisz managers could keep an eagle eye on prices.

They also kept an eye on their captains. "My captains are never to be under the influence of liquor," Carl Laeisz wrote in his instructions; "any contrary information coming to my notice will lead to instant dismissal." At headquarters in Hamburg a secret "captain's book," kept under lock and key, contained candid judgments on each shipmaster—terse appraisals such as "excellent seaman," "top class," "this man to be promoted." Or, less happily, an annotation might read "aggressive," "agitator," even "useless." Presumably, a man deemed to be useless was not given a contract for a second voyage.

The crews that served under Laeisz masters were carefully chosen and watched over, too. A seaman found guilty of an infraction aboard ship—insubordination, say, or falling asleep on watch—had his offense and his punishment (which might be a fine withheld from his wages) entered in the ship's log and read to him before witnesses, who signed the entry. The seaman knew that at the ship's next port of call the contents of the logbook would be transmitted to Laeisz headquarters in Hamburg—and that for repeated misbehavior headquarters might demand dismissal in port. The company maintained a discipline, in short, that was strict but reasonable, and never wantonly cruel.

The natural result of such scrutiny and care was highly skilled and motivated officers and men—and, by the 1890s, a multimillion dollar revenue, the bulk of which came from the Chilean nitrate trade. The Laeisz father and son had made the critical decision to specialize in nitrate in 1867, just at the time when European farmers and manufacturers were beginning to show their voracious appetite for the chemical. And when the Laeiszes gave nitrate their full attention, they brought to the hot, indolent ports of Chile the same thorough efficiency that characterized the running of their ships afloat.

Until the arrival of the Laeisz ships, a lapse of two months was considered a good turnaround time in a Chilean port; a lapse of three was more likely. But the easygoing, mañana philosophy would not do for the hurrying German merchants. First they worked out practical schedules for arrivals and departures—not leaving the matter of sailing up to the whims of their captains. Then, to ensure keeping to those schedules, they stationed permanent German agents in the ports of Pisagua, Iquique, Tocopilla and Tåltal to look after Laeisz interests—if necessary, getting on the good side of local officials by dispensing cases of excellent Hamburg beer.

Among other things, the Laeisz agents contracted for a large and steady supply of lighters—the barges that took cargo to and from the anchored ships in ports where there were no wharves. From the moment the anchor was dropped, P Line crewmen began opening hatches, rigging cargo-handling gear and testing winches. Lighters promptly appeared alongside. Out would come the cargo from Europe, and in would go the nitrates. Then, in a week or 10 days, as the loading neared completion, the ship made ready to sail again; the crew began setting her topsails and moving her slowly out of the roadstead as the final slings of nitrate bags were coming aboard from the last lighter towed alongside. With the P liners monopolizing a port's lighter service in this way whenever they heaved into view, competitors' ships often found themselves waiting untended for days at a time while the German barks unloaded, loaded again and were gone.

Another reason for the advantage the Germans enjoyed was that they devised a way to speed up the stowing of the nitrates in the holds by as much as eightfold. The task of stowing was one that required a surprising amount of skill and judgment. The powdered nitrate solidified on

Swept from her moorings by the norther that lashed the Chilean coast on June 2, 1903, the British windjammer Foyledale wallows helplessly amid her spilled cargo of lumber in Valparaiso harbor while another ship lists on the rocks beyond her and spectators crowd the shoreline to view the wreckage. The fury of this storm, in which some 30 other boats were lost and 90 people perished—among them the Foyledale captain's wife and daughter and six crewmen—is apparent even in this old, clumsily retouched photo.

standing, which virtually eliminated the terrifying possibility of the cargo shifting. But the bags—weighing 200 pounds apiece—had to be artfully positioned for shipping; if they were simply dumped into a hold, their misplaced weight could turn an otherwise seaworthy craft into a dangerously unstable hulk that could not stand up to a storm. So the bags were set in precise pyramids, away from the sides of the ship, a method that positioned the weight along the ship's axis.

The Chilean stevedore designated to construct the pyramid was usually short in height but strong and agile. With a bag on his shoulders, he would trot briskly across the hold until he had reached just the right spot. There would be a sudden, sharp twist to his shoulders and he would nimbly drop the bag precisely in position. It would never have to be moved again. When the vessel arrived at her destination in Europe, the pyramids would have to be broken up with pickaxes, the nitrate powder having solidified en route.

In 30 years of association with European nitrate merchants, the Chilean stevedores learned to guard their talent jealously and insisted on working one stevedore to a ship. That was all well and good for the slower pace of earlier days, when nitrates were not in such demand and sailing ships took their time. But by 1895, even a medium-sized windjammer could carry more than 30,000 bags—a load that would take a lone man almost a month to stow in the hold.

The Laeiszes did not change the basic technique—that was foolproof.

But with compelling persuasion—and undoubtedly numerous well-placed cases of beer—they did succeed in inducing the stevedores to share their skill and increase their numbers, so that six and even eight men would work a ship. At least two men stacked in each hold and all the holds were loaded simultaneously. That single change in operation revolutionized the nitrate trade. Time spent in nitrate ports—at least by P liners—was soon counted in days rather than in weeks or months. Always pressing, always driving, P Line captains would then race back to Hamburg—and begin the cycle anew.

Many of their passages were record breakers. In 1895 the Laeiszes built their first five-master, the marvelous bark Potosi, which had a masterfully designed hull, specially reinforced to bear the punishing weight of 6,000 tons of nitrate in roughly 100,000 cubic feet, a towering mainmast of 212 feet and heavy yards to carry nearly 55,000 square feet of extra-large sails to propel all that weight. Right from the start of her maiden voyage, under the famed Captain Hilgendorf, she won attention for her speed. She sailed out to Chile in an astonishing 66 days; the previous record, made by a French-owned ship, was 74 days, and the average run at the time took roughly 80 days.

Under Hilgendorf and subsequent masters, the Potosi turned in brilliant passages. In 1900, during a record 55-day run to Valparaiso, she set her one-day mark of 378 nautical miles—the equivalent of 435 land miles. Once, she ran for 11 days at an average speed of 11.2 knots, a performance that few vessels ever matched.

Not all a ship's passages could be equally fast, for there was no predicting the weather, but Laeisz windjammers performed with remarkable consistency. While most other such vessels made three round trips to Chile every two years, P liners were making four.

Moreover, P liners were remarkably accident free. In a calling so often associated with distress and disaster, Laeisz ships, built for maximum strength and superbly crewed and maintained, rarely found themselves in serious trouble. Curiously, one of the greatest hazards faced by the P liners—and other swift sailing ships—was caused by the chronic inability of steamship captains to estimate the windjammers' true speed. Steamer captains were forever estimating that these great ships were traveling at a sailing ship's usual six knots instead of the 12 or 14 they were actually making. That kind of mistake could end in a collision, and a heavily traveled sea-lane such as the English Channel could be more perilous at times than the Horn.

For another of the Laeisz firm's illustrious giants, the Preussen, it was all of that. She was a full-rigged five-masted vessel—the only such five-master to be square-rigged on all masts—and a vessel about which superlatives crowd every description (pages 77-80). She may also have been the fastest of the windjammers; though she never raced another ship, she once sailed in a record 57 days from the Channel to Iquique.

But the Preussen sailed for only eight years, from 1902 to 1910. In an awful demonstration of the perils that swift windjammers faced in the English Channel, the Preussen collided in 1910 with a steamer that had miscalculated her speed. She lost her bowsprit and part of her foremast, became unmanageable and eventually drifted onto the rocks near Dover,

The mighty "Preussen," Queen of the Seas

In 1902 the well-known German shipyard of Tecklenborg launched the largest and most sophisticated sailing vessel it had ever built—a five-masted, full-rigged ship built for the Laeisz firm and intended to be the prototype for a new generation of wind-powered superships.

The ship was the mighty *Preussen (below)*, soon to be known around the world as the "Queen of the Seas." She was registered in Lloyd's of London's largest class of ships with an awesome displacement of 11,150 tons. Her gigantic hull measured 440 feet from bow to stern, with a beam of 54 feet and a depth from keel to top deck of 32.6 feet. Yet for all her gargantuan dimensions, she was the model of efficiency and economy. The *Cutty Sark*, most famous of the earlier tea clippers, with 35 crewmen, could carry 1,330 tons of cargo. But the *Preussen*, with 45, could haul almost 8,000 tons.

Moreover, like so many of the windjammers, she showed amazing speed for her vast bulk. With a maximum of 48 sails on and between her five sheet-steel masts—the tallest of which towered 224 feet from keel to truck—the *Preussen* spread 59,000 square feet of canvas. In a stiff wind, these sails would exert a force equal to 6,000 horsepower and drive her through the seas at a surging 17 knots. On one great day in the South Atlantic in 1903, she covered 368 miles in 24 hours for an average speed of almost 15.3 knots.

Even her normal speed of between six and eight knots, depending on the prevailing winds, was as good as most tramp steamers of the day could manage.

As it turned out, the *Preussen* was the only ship of her kind ever built. Advances in the mechanics of steam propulsion in the first decade of the 20th Century, coupled with drastic increases in the cost of construction, made such huge square-riggers a risky investment. Yet the *Preussen* herself might well have served for decades at a good profit had not an unforeseeable stroke of colossal bad luck befallen her only eight years after her launching.

On a hazy night in November 1910, as the *Preussen* was making her way smartly down the English Channel under full sail with a load of pianos bound for Chile, she struck a little British steamer that had miscalculated the *Preussen*'s great speed and tried to slip across her bows—entirely against the rules of the road. The accident happened near the English coast, and the mighty German windjammer, badly damaged at the prow, immediately began a struggle to reach a safe harbor in the teeth of a freshening gale. But she was doomed. With her headgear torn away, she could make no progress into the wind and at 4:30 the following afternoon she was dashed against the rocks just off the Cliffs of Dover and there battered to death.

PREUSSEN

Although the *Preussen* drew her main power from the wind like the oldest ships on the sea, her design and outfitting represented the latest advances in marine technology. To brace her yards—three of which were over 100 feet long—she carried the new hand-operated Jarvis winches at the base of her mainmast, mizzenmast and jigger mast. Her 35,640 feet of standing rigging was all of finest Westphalian steel cable, and another 100,617 feet of running rigging, rove through 1,168 blocks, manipulated her sails.

Two coal-burning boilers, able to recycle their steam, and thus reducing the amount of distilled water carried aboard, were located at the foremast. The boilers powered engines that operated pumps capable of lifting 700 cubic feet of water an hour from her bilges; these same engines operated four winches, which helped haul the yards. So huge was

her rudder that a steam-powered mechanism was installed on her bridge to help turn the great wheel if necessary—although the crew insisted it was scarcely ever used.

The *Preussen* had a midship bridge straddling the deck at the base of the mizzenmast. This superstructure housed the captain and crew, and acted as a breakwater against waves. From the bridge, catwalks ran fore and aft, making the entire deck accessible in even the dirtiest weather.

From the main deck five hatches led below to three enormous levels for cargo: the lower deck, orlop deck and hold. Five open bulkheads—watertight bulkheads would have made loading difficult—ringed the hull at each mast, ensuring rigidity and shouldering some of the pull from the shrouds. A cellular double bottom stiffened the hull and reduced the chances of disaster if she were holed.

1. JIGGER MAST
2. CATWALK
3. MIDSHIP BRIDGE
4. VENTILATOR
5. WARDROOM
6. CAPTAIN'S CABIN
7. FRAMES
8. OFFICERS' CABIN
9. CHARTROOM
10. STEAM ENGINE TO ASSIST STEERING
11. CABLE TO RUDDER QUADRANT
12. WHEEL
13. BINNACLE
14. OFFICERS' WARDROOM

15. MIZZENMAST
16. SAILORS' BERTHS
17. WATER BALLAST
18. BETWEEN-DECK FRAMES
19. JARVIS WINCH
20. HATCH WITH VENTILATOR
21. SAIL STORE
22. GALLEY
23. LOWER DECK
24. LOWER-DECK HATCH
25. CELLULAR BOTTOM
26. FRESH-WATER TANKS
27. SPARE SPAR
28. BILGE PUMP

29. MAINMAST
30. CARGO AND UTILITY DERRICK
31. STEAM-POWERED WINCH
32. MAIN HATCH
33. CAPSTAN
34. DISTILLED-WATER TANK
35. FUEL STORAGE
36. DONKEY PUMP
37. DECK STIFFENERS
38. TRANSVERSE BULKHEAD
39. VERTICAL BOILERS
40. CHIMNEY
41. FOREMAST
42. BITTS

The shaded area above represents the section of the Preussen illustrated on these pages. It includes the midship bridge, the foremast, mainmast, mizzenmast and jigger mast. The fifth mast, not shown below, was commonly called the spanker.

When seen at sea under a full suit of wind-stiffened sails, the *Preussen* was a vision of majesty, but a cross section through her hull just forward of the bridge reveals a most inelegant bargelike shape that was calculated to accommodate the largest possible amount of cargo. Her usual cargo consisted of bags of Chilean nitrate fertilizer, stacked in pyramids so that the ship's center of buoyancy—crucial to its stability—was much higher than it would be had the nitrates been packed wall to wall in the hold as was the practice with lighter cargoes.

The *Preussen*'s outer sheathing was a skin of overlapping steel plates riveted to one another and to the frames of the hull. Similar plating formed the main and lower decks, although the main deck was covered over with a layer of wooden planking.

1. MIZZENMAST
2. CHARTROOM
3. CREW'S QUARTERS
4. GALLEY
5. OFFICERS' QUARTERS
6. LOWER DECK
7. ORLOP DECK
8. HOLD
9. DECK PILLARS
10. STEEL PLATES
11. WATER BALLAST
12. CELLULAR BOTTOM

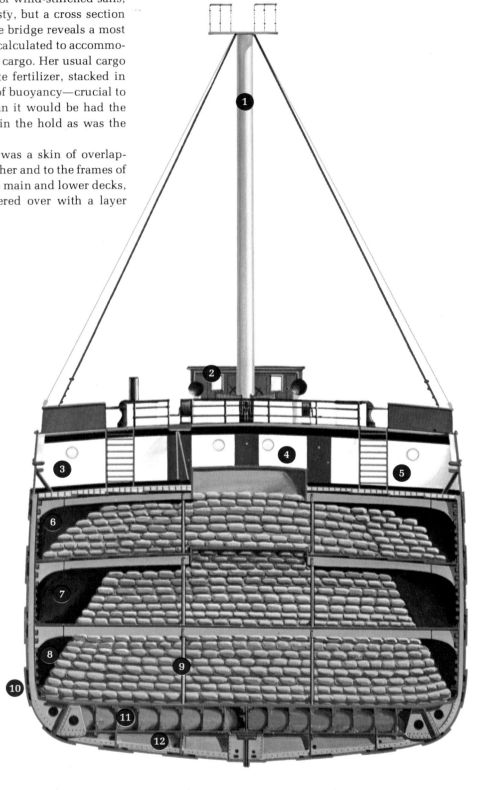

where she later broke up. The combined efforts of several tugs to free her proved futile, and for months afterward she lay a ghostly wreck under the sweeping beacon of the South Foreland lighthouse.

With all their speed and efficiency, the Laeisz ships had only one serious sailing competitor in the nitrate trade: the French firm of Antoine-Dominique Bordes et Fils—another family operation. Antoine, the son of a country doctor, had begun his love affair with ships and the sea in boyhood; he shipped out to Chile at 19 and in 1867, at age 51, became the head of his own fleet of 10 sailing ships. Two years later the Suez Canal opened, obviating the need for steamers to go around Africa, and thus firmly establishing steam on the Mediterranean passages. Undaunted, Bordes risked all his hard-earned capital on 14 iron barks ordered from British yards—and sent them west to Chile.

He entered the market there at more or less the same time that the Laeisz firm was getting started. But the supply of nitrate was seemingly inexhaustible, and there was room enough for both companies in the still-growing market. In the Chilean ports, Bordes adopted many of the same practices as the Laeisz firm, engaging his own lighters and stevedores to ensure service when he needed it. And in other phases of the operation, he added some twists of his own. En route to Chile, several Bordes ships called first at Rio de Janeiro, on the east coast of South America, and delivered coal from Wales for Brazil's brand-new railroad. With no cargo to carry away from Rio for the remaining hazardous passage around the Horn, Bordes ships met the problem of ballast by pumping some 1,500 tons of sea water into specially designed compartments before proceeding on to the Chilean nitrate fields. On arrival there, a mere turn of a wheel would automatically spill the water back into the sea—and the ship would be ready promptly for reloading with a cargo of nitrate.

Bordes vessels were not only efficient working ships, they were sleekly handsome craft, and in some respects seemed to have been designed and fitted out as much for the pleasures of the officers and crew as for cargo carrying. Naturally, French ships must have appropriate French cuisine, with meat or fish twice a day and rations of wine; a 3,000-ton windjammer, for example, would load 15 tons of wine for her crew of 24 on a trip to Chile. They were comfortable: they had long roomy forecastles extending well abaft of the foremast and long poops with spacious charthouses. And they were beautiful, with a color scheme appropriate to their graceful lines: light-gray hulls—a color so distinctive that it was called French gray—white masts and yards, and black-and-white *trompe l'oeil* gunports, a holdover from the days when pirates roamed and it was prudent for sailing ships to look like men-of-war. Few ships matched the beauty of those French vessels. Apprentice William Jones, finding the Bordes *Rhône* tied up with some others in Iquique when he pulled in aboard the homely *British Isles,* was prompted to write: "We were moved to admiration, rather than envy, of such beautiful vessels as these, which really enhanced the prestige of sail, and gave rise to a hope that bigger and better sailing ships would continue to be built."

But beauty was not their only asset. Bordes windjammers were sailed by superb crews, which were a match for the best of the Germans. The Bordes firm—indeed, all French windjammer operators—benefited from a lively interest taken in them by the French government, which believed that a strong merchant marine, both steam and sail, was essential to a strong nation and a strong navy. By government plan, French ships were manned entirely by Frenchmen, down to the deck boys and the scullions, a fact that gave them considerable *esprit de corps*. The government further required the seamen to be reservists in the Navy— and in exchange granted them pensions. A merchant seaman attaining the age of 50, providing he could prove 25 years' service in merchant ships, could look forward to a retirement pension of 600 francs annually.

The French government was beneficent in a number of other, even more vital, ways. In 1881 the government, bent on expanding French foreign trade, began paying subsidies both for ship construction and for voyages. On voyages the bounty for each company was one franc, 70 centimes per gross ton per 1,000 miles sailed—whether or not the ship carried any cargo. That meant that a 3,000-ton ship like the *Jacqueline*, sailing the 15,000-mile passage from France to Australia, could earn a subsidy from the government just for making the trip. It also meant that a French bark could sail long distances in ballast in order to secure a cargo; once at her destination, she could make money on low-paying cargoes— beans, rice, hempseed—that the vessels of other nations tended to avoid. And higher-paying cargoes, such as nitrates, coal and cases of petroleum, were even more profitable for French shippers.

Between the government's handsome subsidies and its own shrewd management, the Bordes firm prospered and the ships proliferated. By 1882, when Antoine's sons, Adolphe, Alexandre and Antonin, had joined the firm, Bordes owned 41 windjammers. Seven of these were giants. The pioneer among them was the *France*, a great five-masted steel bark of 6,200 tons, built especially for the nitrate trade in a British shipyard in 1890. She had an unprecedented four steam winches to each hatch, giving her the ability to discharge 5,000 tons of coal and reload 5,500 tons of nitrate in 11 days. Her sole flaw was an alarming tendency in heavy seas to roll way over and seem to hang virtually on her beam-ends before slowly coming back. But she always did come back, through the worst of the furies of Cape Horn weather, and served her owners with distinction for 11 years in the nitrate trade, giving the best of the Laeisz ships a run for their money.

Indeed, considerable rivalry grew up between the firms, and their ships' crews—half in earnest, half in jest—raced each other's record passages back and forth across the ocean. In 1896 the *France* and Laeisz's *Potosi* made virtually identical voyages. The *France* went out to Iquique in 74 days, the *Potosi* in 75; on the return passage, the *France* came home in 71 days while the *Potosi* made it in 69. Looking on from Paris and Hamburg, respectively, the directors of Bordes and Laeisz encouraged their captains to engage in these races with other ships and awarded them bonuses for winning.

Few other companies stood a chance in such races. Once, when Captain Louis-François Bourgain of the Bordes bark *Hélène* was sitting with several British, German and Italian masters in a café in Iquique, a Ger-

Firm jawed and steady of gaze, Antoine Dominique Bordes was the founder in 1867 of the most illustrious French line of windjammers. Between 1890 and 1920 a total of 127 sailing vessels proudly carried the flag bearing his initials, A. B.

man captain (but not a Laeisz skipper) came in and asked Bourgain if the *Hélène* was scheduled to sail on the following day. When Bourgain said she was, the German offered to bet 500 piasters that his ship would arrive in Hamburg before the *Hélène*. Bourgain haughtily refused: "The captain of the *Hélène* is so sure of arriving first that betting would simply be to rob you." As might have been expected, he got to Hamburg 48 hours before his would-be competitor.

There was, however, a tarnished side to the bright coin minted by the Laeisz and Bordes firms in this era as steam took over more and more of oceangoing commerce. In 1866 there were a dozen or so steam navigation companies engaged in transatlantic trade; by the 1890s the number had nearly doubled and they carried 70 per cent of all cargo. And among the surviving companies still committed to sail, for every Laeisz and Bordes there were dozens of tramp operators, shippers who were so hard-pressed for money that their vessels were chronically run down, their captains repeatedly ill-chosen, their seamen poorly treated. Grief and hardship was the universal lot of those condemned to serve on such hellships, as they were called.

On ships where penny pinching was the order of the day, the effects ranged from comic to criminal. One second mate remembered reporting for duty on the windjammer *Terpsichore* in 1910, arriving just as the officers were having tea with the captain and his wife. Invited to join them, the new man picked up a biscuit and prepared to butter it. He was brought up short by a command from the captain's wife, who snapped, "Turn that biscuit over!" In his bewilderment, it took him a moment to realize that he had been about to butter the split side of the biscuit. The crusty side, being smooth, would not take so much butter. He dutifully applied the butter as instructed—and declined to sail with the ship when she left port.

A more serious form of parsimony took place during a 1908 passage made from Portland, Oregon, to Liverpool by the British windjammer *Wavertree*. The owners provisioned her with only enough food for three and a half months—in full knowledge that the passage would take almost six. After the ship's canned meat was used up, all hands—including the officers—subsisted on three biscuits a day. Then the biscuits ran out and the crew began boiling wheat taken from the grain cargo. Meanwhile, coal for the galley stove, also in short measure, ran out and all surplus lumber on the ship, including a spare spar, was chopped up and burned for fuel. After weeks on end of a diet of nothing but wheat gruel, many of the crew developed scurvy and the captain had to abolish the watches—adding neglect of the ship's safety to the miseries of the sick and famished crew. Not until they were within three days of Liverpool did the crew find blessed relief; a fishing smack was sighted, and sold the *Wavertree* some of the haul. Seldom was fish so welcome to a windjammer crew. "We had two meals of fish that day, and another for breakfast the next day," one of them remembered.

A mean or badly managed firm naturally attracted like-minded captains, who in turn were poorly paid and often proved disastrous—both for the owners they served and for the benighted crews under them.

Flying the French tricolor, the A. B. flag of the House of Bordes, and a blue and white banner signifying that she is due to leave port, the Hélène rides to anchor in Nantes while a sailor bids his girl au revoir. Bordes's ships were so sleek and graceful that a seaman chancing upon one at sea was moved to exclaim: "It seemed crude to think of a gutful of coal being carried in so much loveliness."

Many such masters resorted to cheating and chicanery as the only way to get by. They manipulated accounts, billed some items twice, took kickbacks from suppliers and sometimes charged their ship's account for badly needed maintenance items that were never ordered at all. And as the captain went, so went the crew—the mates, the seamen, the occasional apprentices all cheating and stealing whenever the opportunity presented itself.

Coal cargoes were especially easy to manipulate, particularly at Chilean ports. The trick was to hoodwink the Chilean tally clerk who had been assigned to witness the unloading. An apprentice "helping" the clerk might place his foot surreptitiously on the scale while the bags were weighed. Or the clerk might be invited to go on board the windjammer for a convivial drink of *picso* and perhaps a short siesta while the mate took over the tallying. When the stipulated tonnage had been tallied, noted one observer, "it was strange that there still remained 50 or more tons of coal in the hold. Perhaps the pit weights supplied at our loading port had been incorrect? Who could tell?" The coal that was remaining in the hold would be sold later by the men who had conspired to tip the scales, with no questions asked by the buyer.

More imaginative was a scheme that apprentice William Jones happened to witness when his full-rigged ship the *British Isles* went on from Chile to Australia. Standing on deck one evening in the port of Newcastle, he noticed the mate of a nearby ship carefully coiling a long length of mooring line on the deck. This was an unusual activity for a ship's officer, so Jones kept watching. When the mate had finished with his coiling, he lowered an end of the rope over the rail and down to the water's edge. That done, he went ashore.

Jones was still on deck aboard his own ship about an hour later, when two men in a motorboat came quietly alongside the ship. By now the light was too dim for Jones to tell if the mate was among them; presumably he was. In any case, one of the men seized the loose rope while the other manned the wheel. Soon some 90 fathoms—540 feet—of expensive line had uncoiled without a hitch and was trailing behind the boat as it made off toward shore, where it would be sold to the master of another ship, or perhaps even be sold back to the ship from which it had been stolen. Jones later learned that such thefts were common in Newcastle—and, in fact, in just about any other port.

Thieving officers might abuse only their ships' owners. But drinking

A windjammer flying the British Red Ensign gets a helpful nudge from two paddle-wheel tugs at the entrance to Dunkirk harbor, home port to the Bordes windjammers, one of which lies at her berth. By the turn of the century, when this photograph was taken, the Bordes firm had moved its main operations from Nantes, upriver on the Loire, to the booming port of Dunkirk on the English Channel— the better to disperse nitrate cargoes to the farmers of northern Europe.

ones were often dangerous, and intolerably hard on shipmates who had to live with them for months on end. The astounding story of a round-the-world voyage made by the British bark *Penrhyn Castle* was related years later by the man who served on her as second mate, Claude Wool-lard. He felt such shame for his captain that he never mentioned the man's name in his entire account.

The ship was no sooner under way from Melbourne, Australia, for Callao, Peru, with a cargo of grain than the captain and the mate began drinking heavily. On the second night out, the ship ran into a terrible gale. As she wallowed through the seas with no one to command her, most of her sails blew out. Then her cargo shifted and she rolled over almost onto her beam-ends. Her lower yards touched the water, and heavy seas washed perilously over the deck. The captain, in a drunken terror, now lost his senses altogether. He invited the crew to take refuge with him in the sail locker, and there he passed around whiskey to all those who crowded in with him.

Only the clear heads, valiant courage and dogged perseverance of Second Mate Woollard and three apprentices saved the vessel. Declin-ing the captain's offer, these four lashed themselves to the wheel and the rigging and stayed on deck all night. There, despite being drenched by the combers that crashed across the tossing ship, they managed to keep the head of the listing, crippled vessel more or less into the wind and waves. Once during the night the sodden captain appeared and stag-gered toward the wheel, only to lose his balance, slide along the lee rail and beat a stumbling retreat back belowdecks.

At daybreak the storm eased, and one of the apprentices went below to report to the captain that the worst seemed over. But the captain was sprawled on a settee in the saloon. He was out cold; so were the mate and the rest of the crew. Not until late afternoon did they show signs of life. For the next two days the captain oversaw the tedious shifting of the cargo back into place—and then returned to the bottle, as did the mate and the crew. Once again Woollard found himself carrying out the du-ties of both captain and mate, not only at sea but afterward, when the ship reached port.

For four months the *Penrhyn Castle* lay off a hot, disagreeable Pe-ruvian island, taking on a cargo of guano. There was scarcely a day when the officers and the bulk of the crew did not drink themselves into a stupor. During one roaring binge the captain went berserk and tried to jump overboard; he was saved from drowning only because some fast-moving seamen pulled him back and held him under a pile of wet jackets until he quieted down.

Almost every day there was a vicious brawl. One sailor who was bested in a fight in the fo'c's'le had his hands and feet tied and then was hoisted, feet first, high into the rigging. There he swung all through the tropic afternoon. No officer came to his aid. It was taboo for officers to interject themselves into these fo'c's'le fights unless a man's life was in danger. So Woollard stayed out of it, and the first mate, drunk as always, spent the afternoon firing off the vessel's distress rockets. Short-ly thereafter, the mate collapsed and was packed ashore to a hospital with delirium tremens.

A bold Yankee challenge to the steamships

"Our family has been in the business of constructing and sailing ships since 1823, and I claim to understand it in all its bearings as well as anyone in the country." So declared Maine shipbuilder Arthur Sewall in 1894, when he launched his *Dirigo*, the first steel square-rigged vessel to be built in the United States.

To the crusty Sewall, the prospect of foreign-built windjammers monopolizing the shipping of American cargo by sail was a disgrace. Thus, at a time when most American shipyards began to build steamships, A. Sewall & Co. mounted the sole American shipbuilding effort to compete with the great steel square-riggers of Europe.

To construct the *Dirigo* (named after the state of Maine's Latin motto, "I lead"), Sewall relied heavily on Great Britain; he imported plans, a superintendent and even the steel hull plates. But the next Sewall ship, the *Erskine M. Phelps*, launched in 1898, was Yankee from stem to stern.

By the time Sewall died in 1900, his shipyard had built six steel windjammers, and it went on to build three more to carry cargoes of American-produced grain, oil and coal, and sugar from the U.S. territory of Hawaii to ports around the world. In 1905 Sewall's son and nephew even considered building an enormous five-masted steel bark to rival the great German nitrate ships *Potosi* and *Preussen*.

However, their five-master was never built; over the next few decades steamships ate deeply into the windjammer trade, and inevitably Sewall's business suffered. Increasingly also, the company suffered from a lack of experienced crews. "There is nobody that wants to go in square rig," said the master of the *Edward Sewall*, stranded in Norfolk, Virginia, in February 1916. By the year's end, the Sewalls had sold the last of their steel ships.

Known as "the Maritime Prince," shipbuilder Arthur Sewall had ambitions beyond success with windjammers; in 1896 he was William Jennings Bryan's Vice-Presidential running mate in the great Populist's losing bid for the White House.

The flag-bedecked Edward Sewall raises smoke from the friction as she slides down the ways into Maine's Kennebec River on October 3, 1899. A crack heavy-weather sailer, the four-masted bark made a number of smart voyages under the Sewall flag, including one run from Honolulu to Philadelphia, some 15,000 miles, that she made in 107 days.

Somehow or other, despite this incredible donnybrook, the guano was eventually loaded. Hiring a replacement for the hospitalized mate, the captain had the sense, or the luck, to secure an excellent onetime captain named Owens, who had a talent for imposing discipline. Under his firm hand, the ship's mood changed abruptly. With Owens in virtual command, the *Penrhyn Castle* sailed to Antwerp, where the captain was instantly dismissed.

A captain who was purely mean could be even worse than a master who drank. One such was T. E. L. Tindale, a cruel and capricious man who from 1904 to 1906 had command of the four-masted British bark *Inverness-shire* on an ill-fated voyage around the world.

No one was spared from this man's evil wrath. Before the ship had been a few weeks out of London, Tindale, in a peevish fit, demoted his second mate. Next his ire fell upon the third mate, whom he put in irons. In Valparaiso, where the ship docked to discharge a cargo of coal, the apprentices lodged a formal protest with the captain, saying they were overworked; Tindale responded by ordering them to move out of their quarters with the officers aft and into the fo'c's'le, where the ordinary seamen slung their hammocks. The apprentices pointed out that this was in direct violation of their terms of employment; Tindale responded by putting them on bread and water while requiring them to help unload 4,000 tons of coal. When the vessel arrived at Iquique to load a cargo of nitrates, 12 of the crew refused to work on the ground that the food was poor; Tindale put them in irons. By the time the *Inverness-shire* reached home port in England, the ship had experienced an incredible 87 crew

Rusted and scarred by the arduous passage around Cape Horn, two windjammers—the Rochambeau (center), 173 days from London, and the William P. Frye (far right), 139 days from Baltimore—lie among ferries and steamers at San Francisco's bustling Howard Street pier in 1908. Hundreds of windjammers unloaded their cargoes each year at San Francisco; the city was the world's third busiest port in the early 20th Century.

changes—and the incumbents were refusing duty altogether. The owners finally fired Captain Tindale.

Sadly, such tales of mindless mismanagement abounded on sailing ships, for it was a harsh, perilous world that brought out either the best in men or the worst. On the American bark *Commodore T. H. Allen* in 1889, a seaman who talked back to the bullying third mate was thrown against the rail by the mate so violently that his shoulder was dislocated. When he appealed to the captain, he was confined; the only treatment for his shoulder was a dose of salts. A cruel French master, known in Nantes as *Oiseau Noir*, or "Blackbird," once became so infuriated at his own 18-year-old son, who was serving aboard his ship, that he climbed down into the hold and landed a vicious kick on his son's head. On the ships of a Hamburg company, young seamen were made to remove their shirts in bitterly cold weather simply to test their fortitude. A young Dane, crossing the equator for the first time on the German bark *Osterbek,* took part in what started out as a conventional King Neptune celebration (*page 55),* but that soon turned into a torture ceremony. The youth was repeatedly keelhauled—dragged under the keel of the ship. This barbarous form of hazing often ended in death. The ship's officers made no attempt to intervene.

Seamen who endured such abuses had little hope of redress, even when they reached port, for the laws tended to favor the ships' officers, regardless of who was in the right. In San Francisco, a port notorious for its corruption, local officials and law enforcement authorities, bribed by shipping interests, ignored the criminal acts of captains, even when a rare seaman had the nerve to lodge a complaint. But in due course San Francisco was also the scene of some of the earliest successful attempts to establish legal rights for seamen.

The achievement was largely the work of the fledgling Sailors' Union of the Pacific, which was organized in 1891. Soon the union was publishing a newspaper with a column called the "Red Record," written by a young Scottish windjammer sailor named Walter Macarthur, who recounted several case histories of shipboard brutality that, though brought to court, went shockingly unpunished. Among Macarthur's revelations: that the first mate of the square-rigger *Henry B. Hyde*, charged with having broken a seaman's wrist with a belaying pin, was exonerated on the ground of "justifiable discipline"; that the 260-pound second mate of the bark *Tam O'Shanter*, charged with biting chunks out of one man's hand and arm, and kicking another from aloft, was acquitted also, on the ground of "justifiable discipline"; that a certain Captain Nickels of the *May Flint*, accused of beating a seaman with a holystone, a heavy chunk of rock about the size and shape of a Bible and used for polishing decks, was allowed to go free; that the case of Captain Azecheus Allen of the bark *Benjamin F. Packard*, who ordered his first mate and the carpenter to assault a seaman he had shackled in irons, was dismissed "for lack of evidence" despite the testimony of several of the crew.

Reprinted in daily newspapers, the "Red Record" reports shocked not only the lay public but a good many shipowners as well. Still, remedies were slow in coming. Not until 1915, some 25 years after the first aborted efforts of the Sailors' Union, did Congress pass legislation making ships' captains accountable for their actions aboard, and shipowners accountable for their captains. Both could be subject to fines for cruel and irresponsible treatment of the seamen in their charge. The legislation applied to all kinds of seagoing vessels, not just windjammers, of course. But it was the appalling practices existing on some windjammers that precipitated the action, and it was windjammer sailors who finally managed to push the reforms through.

In the days before they received legal protection, the luckless crews of hellships, of whatever nation, had only two recourses. One was desertion—and that was a remedy that had to wait until the ship reached port. The other was mutiny.

Few mutinies were attempted. A man could be imprisoned for simple insubordination. And should a captain or mate be killed by a sailor, no matter the circumstances, the man faced certain hanging. Yet in the harsh world of the windjammers, the threat of mutiny was ever present.

Captains knew that—and took precautions for their own safety. They required seamen reporting on board to relinquish all weapons except knives, which were needed for seamen's work. They generally avoided being alone with any crew member of questionable behavior, and they and their mates kept revolvers handy just in case.

That precaution could work against them, as happened on board the British windjammer *Leicester Castle*, sailing from San Francisco to Queenstown, Ireland, with a cargo of grain and a couple of troublemakers. What triggered these men to action is lost to history, but it is not difficult to imagine that the skipper, Captain R. D. Peattie, must have been a hard man, as most windjammer masters had to be, and that his sailors were poorly fed, overworked, underpaid and nursing any number of other grievances.

Whatever the reasons, on the night of September 2, 1902, Peattie was roused in his cabin by a seaman named Sears, who said that a man had fallen from the rigging. As Peattie was about to go out the port door of the cabin to investigate, Sears blocked his way, whereupon an accomplice named Hobbs entered the cabin through the starboard door, exclaiming, "Now, then, Captain!" Peattie turned around to face the voice, and Hobbs shot him in the chest with a revolver stolen from the second mate. Peattie, despite his wound, lunged for Hobbs, who fired again, this time hitting the captain in the arm.

By now the gunfire had attracted attention, bringing shipmates to the scene. The first to arrive was the second mate; Hobbs fired and killed him. Next, two sailors showed up, whereupon Hobbs and Sears lost their nerve and fled. At last the first mate arrived and took charge. Calling all hands aft, he asked them to help search for Hobbs and Sears. Shortly after midnight, somebody saw a makeshift raft with three men aboard—Hobbs, Sears and an unidentified companion—floating past the ship. Presumably the three men had jumped ship, being more willing to face the lonely terrors of the ocean than the hangman's noose. By morning the raft had vanished, and the three were never heard of again. As for Captain Peattie, that stalwart recovered from his wounds and was back on the poop in a few days. The moral of the story, which most sailors thoroughly understood, was that a lone malcontent, or even several disaffected men, almost never had a chance against their officers backed by loyalists among the crew.

Even in the face of a crew united in mutiny, the rebellion might be squelched—or at least neutralized—by a show of forbearance. Such was the case on the British ship *Monkbarns*, bound for New York with a consignment of wheat for the United States Army during World War I. For three tense months, 76-year-old Captain J. Donaldson held a fractious crew at bay as the ship made the 12,000-mile passage from Melbourne, Australia, around the Horn to the east coast of South America, through waters infested with German submarines.

The crew, a motley and discontented lot from the start, were loudest on the subject of the food, which, for the owners, was harder to get than usual because of wartime shortages. They complained, not without some justice, that the potatoes were black and the peas as hard as stones. But that sort of fare was common enough on windjammers, and scarcely cause for six seamen to storm the poop one day and seize Captain Donaldson in the chartroom. Slamming him onto the table, they announced their refusal to work and threatened to carve him up with their knives if he did not improve the food.

At that point, the *Monkbarns'* mates rushed in to rescue Donaldson. The skipper made an effort to reason with his assailants. Clearly he would not be able to replace the food at sea. But it was equally obvious that he could not sail his 1,700-ton windjammer if two thirds of the crew were languishing in irons. Promising to lay in a store of better food upon arrival in the first possible port, Donaldson at length persuaded the men to return to their work.

The mutineers grudgingly assented to the captain's request. But as the weeks went by, though there was no more violence, they increasingly soldiered at their jobs—even when that meant putting the ship and their own lives in peril. In the darkness of 2 o'clock one morning, for instance, the sudden appearance of an iceberg required a quick change of course. The mutineers sullenly braced the yards as they were ordered to do—and then rushed for the lifeboats. Only because the officers ordered them back at gunpoint did they remain on deck as the *Monkbarns* narrowly missed a collision.

After the ship had rounded the Horn, she faced warmer weather and fair winds along the east coast of South America. It was therefore necessary to grease the masts for easy hoisting and lowering of the yards. But by this time, discipline had so completely and irrevocably broken down

Treasures of timber from Puget Sound

Snow-covered square-riggers and schooners dock at Port Blakely, Washington, in the winter of 1905 to load cargoes of wood.

that officers were climbing aloft to do that menial chore themselves.

At last, Captain Donaldson was in range of Rio de Janeiro, and so he flew a distress signal. When the ship reached Rio, a detachment from a British guard ship was on hand to take command of the situation.

Donaldson's lonely heroism won him mixed reactions from the authorities. Critics argued that he should have put the offenders in irons after the first breach of discipline. Supporters pointed out that averting bloodshed and bringing the ship successfully around the perilous Horn and her cargo safely to port was an extraordinary achievement. The upshot was that he was forgiven—and sent back out for another voyage on the *Monkbarns*. He eventually retired to Melbourne and lived to the ripe old age of 90.

But punishment was in store for the five ringleaders of mutinous crewmen, who were dealt with, as expected, by court-martial at the British consulate in Rio, then shipped back to England. There they

"Thick as the hair on a dog's back, reaching to God's elbow," was the way the first settlers in the Pacific Northwest described the awesome stands of Douglas fir trees ringing Washington's Puget Sound. They at first cursed the mountainous, unfarmable timberland as a "green desert." But soon they came to appreciate the logging potential of the virgin forests growing within a spar's reach of the deep waters of the Sound. In a few decades' time, a great industry had grown up, shipping lumber across the oceans to the farthest reaches of the world.

For windjammers, it was an ideal trade. In comparison with some of the unprotected roadsteads off the coasts of Peru, Chile and Australia, where windjammers loaded guano, nitrates, coal and wheat, the waters of Puget Sound were a placid haven in which to load cargoes. The entrance to the Sound was via the sheltered Strait of Juan de Fuca, while the Sound itself harbored hundreds of fine anchorages and sites for docks.

By the 1890s, in the harbors of Seattle, Port Blakely and Tacoma, where crews loaded lumber around the clock seven days a week, sailing ships clustered three and four deep at the docks. In Port Townsend, recalled a sailor, the seamen's boardinghouse became a "regular League of Nations," with old salts from every corner of the world gathered in the common room.

By the turn of the century, Puget Sound mills were shipping over 500 million board feet of lumber annually to markets from Shanghai to Hamburg. Cargoes ranged from shiploads of low-grade railroad ties to select bundles of deck planking (12 inches wide and absolutely free of knots).

Despite the enormous demand in the eastern United States, bulk shipments to the Atlantic seaboard were low until the 1890s. With the 15,000-mile voyage around Cape Horn to New York or Philadelphia, a windjammer took almost a year to deliver a single shipment and return.

Then, in 1893, the Great Northern Railroad completed its transcontinental line to Seattle. Lumber mills turned increasingly to the railroads, and by 1906, shipments by land surpassed those by windjammers, although the tall masts of the lumber ships could still be counted on Puget Sound until the late 1920s.

Crewmen of the four-masted bark Lynton, moored stern first at Port Blakely harbor, load bundled boards up wooden ramps. "The narrow cove at Port Blakely was a harbor known to sailormen from Antwerp to Sydney," recalled one observer.

were marched off the gangplank in handcuffs and sent straight to jail. So ended the *Monkbarns* mutiny—the last one ever to be recorded on a British sailing ship.

Although mutiny was rare, desertion was not. Seamen who had sailed under brutal captains and mates lost no time in deserting the moment they reached port. Many another sailor deserted his vessel for no better reason than that jumping ship seemed to be part of a seaman's nature. The *British Isles,* the windjammer on which apprentice William Jones had arrived off Pisagua that day in 1905, was a generally well-run vessel. But Jones had no sooner begun to lend a hand in the port duty—unloading the 3,600-ton cargo of coal—than he discovered a fact of seafaring life. "At turn-to time on the third day, three able seamen were missing," Jones wrote. "As day followed day, more men deserted, without waiting to collect their wages. At last only two men remained in the forecastle—out of an original 20."

Desertion was a widespread phenomenon on ships of virtually every nationality. Only the best of the German operators—such as the Laeisz firm—and the highly subsidized and motivated French were more or less free of the problem.

For some sailors, many a thrumming port held the promise of good jobs ashore. Lumberjacking in Portland, Oregon, and ranching inland from Melbourne, for instance, paid nearly $40 a month at a time when the average pay aboard British ships was about $14. But the vast majority of deserting seamen climbed right back aboard another ship. Every waterfront the world over had taverns and boardinghouses that not only welcomed the seamen's patronage but served as recruiting centers for most of the ships in the harbor. In long-established European ports such as Hamburg, Rotterdam and Liverpool, such places were generally respectable and honest. But in rough-and-tumble boomtowns like San Francisco and Melbourne, for every boardinghouse operator who was honest, there were dozens more whose crimps—so called from a German word meaning "hook"—acted like the infamous naval press gangs of yore, scouring the docks, luring men to desert and often forcibly shanghaiing sailors onto another ship.

So bold and tough were the crimps that they frequently swarmed on board an incoming vessel even before she had dropped anchor. John Mason, who served an apprenticeship aboard a British windjammer, described the arrival of the *Marlborough Hill* in San Francisco while he was there.

"We could see the boats putting out from the shore long before she got near the anchorage," he wrote. "Those were the boarding house runners and crimps looking for men. We could see the mates and apprentices trying their level best to prevent them from getting on board; if they were prevented in one place they would swarm on board in another part of the ship. As the chain was rattling out through the hawse-pipes, bags were going over the side into the crimps' boats, and before the ship was properly moored all her sailors were in the boats making for the water-front, all merry; we could see the bottle of old Kentucky being passed around in the boats. By the time these men

The perils of sailors who fall prey to crooked boardinghouse keepers and other evil types in port are dramatized in these illustrations from an 1873 article entitled "Jack Ashore" in Harper's New Monthly Magazine. At top, Jack is bullied into accompanying a touter and his confederate to a seaman's boardinghouse. Once inside, Jack finds himself buying drink after drink for "a cluster of repulsive women" until his bill is so large that he must ship out posthaste on a departing vessel in order to pay his debts.

reached the waterfront they would be dead drunk, and on board an outward-bound ship before morning, with three months' wages gone."

The crimps would begin by offering the arriving seamen, for a fee, cushy berths on another ship—a promise not hard to believe if the men had just come in on a hellship. If fast talk and free-flowing whiskey failed, the crimps resorted to drugs and beatings—anything that would allow them to supply another ship's captain with a crew.

A lone seaman who refused to desert was often helpless in the face of the crimps. But a band of determined and loyal sailors could usually beat them off. An apprentice serving on the British windjammer *Blackbraes* when she sailed into San Francisco at the turn of the century recalled being asked to lend an older crew member his knife. "It was a special one, with an eight-inch steel blade which could not close without opening the catch. When asked why he wanted it, he informed me that the boardinghouse masters and their bullies were expected to come on board that night and the crew intended to fight them off. Handing it over, I wished him good luck. We apprentices were told to keep out of the way and we therefore spent the night in a safe place ashore. Next morning, when the knife was handed back, I noticed stains on it, and was told that it had been very useful in helping to beat the bullies off."

But if incoming captains detested the preying crimps, outgoing ones often found themselves conspiring in the practice, willy-nilly. With their ships emptied by desertion and other misfortunes, they had to turn to the crimps for a new crew. And so the crimps profited at both ends. First they extracted one to three months' wages from the seamen they had recruited or kidnaped and robbed. Then, when they delivered their quarry, outfitted with oilskins, sea boots and straw mattresses, to a ship making ready to depart, the desperate captain would pay them handsomely in blood money. The sum varied according to supply and demand; in the early 1900s it ranged from about $50 per man in Pisagua, where there were few shoreside lures for seamen, to $120 in Portland, where the lumber camps beckoned and seamen were in shorter supply.

Once he had paid the blood money for the men, it was up to the captain to hold onto his newly assembled crew—and the devil take the skipper who relaxed his vigilance. William Jones recalled that, when his captain signed on a new crew the night before sailing from Pisagua, the new recruits were kept under guard by the mate while the apprentices did all the work of making ready to sail. John Mason, observing a similar scene in San Francisco, explained the reason. "It was nothing unusual," he wrote, "for a crimp to put men on board in the morning, steal them again at night, take them to another ship, and get another 60 dollars' blood money for them."

Crimping was such a lucrative profession that a famous Portland crimp named Larry Sullivan, a brutal onetime prize fighter, was known to have made $80,000 in three years, a huge fortune for those days. With that as a stake, Sullivan built himself a magnificent mansion in the most fashionable part of town and went on to become a millionaire mining broker. But windjammer men everywhere were gratified when Larry the Crimp eventually overreached himself, went broke and died a pauper, ragged and alone.

Girding for the fight for survival

The tempest was the windjammer's constant companion. No sea was free of storms; even the languid Mediterranean could turn terrible when the hot summer siroccos blew up from the south, and ships could disappear without a trace in France's Bay of Biscay. But in the Southern oceans, where the windjammers plied their trade, foul weather seemed to come more often and with greater ferocity than in the Northern Hemisphere. The waters were in almost continual turmoil off southern Australia and Africa's Cape of Good Hope, and in the roaring forties guarding South American coasts. At Cape Horn, screaming winds, pounding waves, and pelting rains, sleet and snow combined in the vilest conditions the world had to offer.

A prudent windjammer skipper never relaxed his guard. The basic rule of survival, as one captain put it, was to "prepare thoroughly for the fight beforehand." At the first sign of a storm, crews were sent aloft to replace fair-weather sails with heavy-duty canvas. When the barometer began to drop, sail was furled, rigging repaired, footropes renewed, and life lines strung fore and aft. "On the thoroughness with which a single piece of line is set," a captain said, "men's lives and the safety of the entire vessel may hang."

In the series of detailed etchings on these pages, marine artist Arthur Briscoe captured the meticulous preparations, then the desperate battle itself. Done during the 1920s and 1930s, Briscoe's illustrations testify to the supreme efforts of the crews—underscoring one sailor's comment that "in the sailing of a big ship in foul weather there is a remarkable force of some kind that makes ordinary men surpass themselves in feats of strength, effectiveness and daring."

Under a tropical sun, a seaman overhauls one of the lines in anticipation of stormy days. The crew paid close attention to the condition of the footropes beneath the yards. "They must be so strong," said one captain, "that nothing shall break though 30 men swing upon the footrope while the torn sail thunders."

Sailors attend to the waterproofing of the deck, using mallets and caulking irons to drive a tarred rope fiber, called oakum, between the planking. Molten pitch, poured into the seams, completed the job. Besides decks, hatch covers were caulked against the expected deluge.

In the calm before the storm, a new topgallant sail puts up no fight as sailors balance 100 feet aloft, bending the canvas to the yard. In anticipation of fierce gales, patched sails—useful enough in fair weather—were replaced by a heavy-duty suit made from canvas so stiff and unyielding that it was known in fo'c's'le lingo as "the nun's shift."

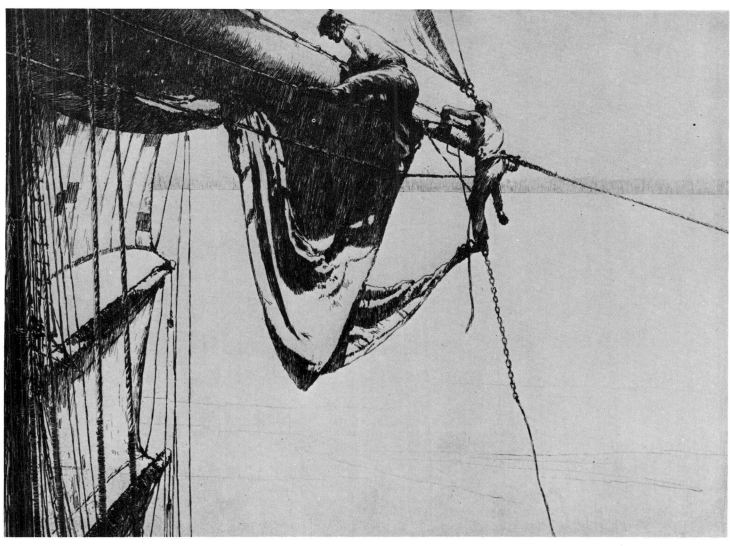

As the seas begin to buck and ramp, a captain takes his post at the weather rail to match wits with the rising winds. Throughout one storm in the roaring forties, the windjammer Arethusa's captain kept that post for 36 hours, eliciting from an awed apprentice the observation that, when the grim sport demanded, the captain "seemed able to do without food or sleep indefinitely."

Peering through sextants, a captain and his mate calculate the angle of the sun to fix the ship's position as accurately as possible before a storm. In tempest-tossed oceans, a captain might go for weeks without a celestial fix; indeed, at the tip of South America, said one sailor, "four ships out of five rounded Fury Island without their masters really knowing they had reached the area of the Horn."

Grasping taut life lines prudently strung in advance, a storm-racked crew manages to stay upright though green seas tumble across a rolling deck. In addition to life lines, safety nets were frequently hung above the bulwarks. Serving as rope seines, they collected men as though they were fish when the waters rushed over the rails and back to the sea.

Crewmen struggle to secure a lifeboat torn from its lashings by the wrenching fingers of the sea. Equipment and boats were not all that was tied down: during an especially violent storm, crew members might spend the entire watch lashed to the rails or masts to perform their duties.

Their bellies to the yard and their heels to the footrope, three sailors grab for a topsail that has torn loose from its gaskets. A storm-tattered sail might be salvaged if ropes could be lashed around it in time. But all too often, as one sailor recalled, the effort produced only the sorry sight of the shredded canvas "flying to leeward to be swallowed in the welter of foam and spindrift."

Knee-deep in swirling water and drenched to the skin, three sailors strain at the bilge pump on deck. A good pump could lift water from belowdecks at the rate of a ton a minute. In a severe storm, with green water constantly crashing on board, the bilge pumps had to be manned virtually without cessation.

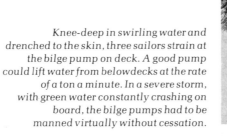

Snugged down to her main lower topsail, a windjammer lies hove to, outriding the worst blasts the elements have to offer.

Chapter 4

Cape Horn: where the wild gales raged

Her sails in rags, the French windjammer Jean has only a jib and topsail to carry her through the Cape Horn fury in this painting of a 1908 passage.

n an endless procession the glassy gray-blue mountains are marching from the west. From their summits blow flapping manes of blinding spray, which the storm tears to shreds. The black-gray clouds are balled deep. A whole hellish concert roars in the rigging. Rushing come the seas over the port rail, strike the deck threateningly, wash in a fury around hatches and capstans and run off gurgling through the wash ports. A universal roaring fills the air that seems to stop up the ears as if with sand. No one can make himself understood except by shouting full strength into another's ear. When the squalls strike, a man must turn his head away in order to breathe at all. The excessive pressure of air forces itself through mouth and nose into the body, blows up the lungs until they are no longer in condition to breathe out. At times, rain and hail showers come down, then a strange hissing and singing mingles with the roaring of the storm. The air is gray with flying water and opaque as milk glass."

The words are those of Hermann Piening, captain of the four-masted German bark *Peking* in the 1920s, describing the conditions that men and ships routinely faced rounding Cape Horn at the tip of South America. It was a terrible place for any sailor in any kind of vessel. In the 1850s and 1860s the clippers had suffered greatly while turning the Horn on their passages to the American West Coast with their human cargoes of gold seekers, and many were lost to the tempests. But the clippers nevertheless had an easier time of it than the windjammers, for which Cape Horn held a special agony.

To be sure, the windjammers were constructed of steel and were far stronger than the wooden-hulled clippers. Yet their slab-sided hulls were less fine-lined than those of the clean little clippers and took a heavier beating from the seas; deeply laden with their enormous cargoes, the windjammers tended to slam sickeningly through the seas rather than rise gracefully to the waves. Always more difficult to sail than the nimble clippers, the windjammers also paid a heavy price for their smaller crews; the 20 to 30 men they carried could not adjust sails to cope with weather changes as rapidly as the 50- to 60-man complements on board the earlier clippers.

Rounding the Horn in a windjammer was a frightful and exhausting experience. A sailor from Australia named Ken Attiwill, who made the journey in 1929, described the area with passionate loathing as a "treacherous, tempestuous, awful place—cold, deserted, and utterly miserable." Even some of the names of its prominent features reflect its forbidding nature: Desolate Bay, Deceit Island, Mistaken Cape, Fury Harbor, Hately Bay, Dislocation Harbor. As the great Laeisz shipmaster Robert Miethe put it, "Cape Horn is a place where the devil made the biggest mess he could."

This devil's mess is itself nothing more than a tiny island, no more than five miles long, a dying, drowning upthrust of the great Andes mountain range before it plunges into the Southern ocean. Below the Strait of Magellan the frigid, fog-locked archipelago of Tierra del Fuego disintegrates into forlorn islands that, sweeping southeastward for 200 miles, grow smaller and smaller until they are mere dabs on the charts.

The last of these is Cape Horn, a grim, steep-sided, volcanic baffle between the Atlantic and the Pacific. It stands at lat. 55° 59′ S., long. 67° 16′ W., of the Greenwich meridian—and it is the uttermost point of the Americas.

The bleak and barren landmark was first sighted in 1616 by a barrel-shaped Dutch captain, Willem Schouten of Hoorn, Holland, who was seeking to break through to the Pacific by some route other than Magellan's tortuous strait or the time-consuming passage around Africa's Cape of Good Hope. Heading south and west, Schouten and his little 360-ton *Unity* first sailed through the 14-mile sea corridor between Tierra del Fuego and a large island northeast of its tip. Schouten called the island Staten Island, after the States-General, then his country's ruling body, and named the passageway the Strait of Le Maire, after a testy old Amsterdam merchant named Isaac Le Maire, the expedition's chief backer. Emerging from the strait, Schouten encountered "mighty waves that came rolling along before the wind"—a dire greeting from Cape Horn, which still lay many miles to the southwest and soon appeared off the *Unity*'s starboard bow.

Gazing at the forbidding cliffs amid the froth of the wild sea, Schouten suddenly understood where he was. "It *is* the last point between the seas," he said, and then in a rush of emotion he decided to name it after the tidy Dutch town whence he came. "Cape Hoorn!" he cried. "Cape Hoorn!"

For more than three centuries, men in sailing ships followed Schouten's route and found it fearsome. The Strait of Le Maire, a shortcut—for those masters who dared risk it—to the Horn from the east, was itself formidable, as Captain Piening of the *Peking* later eloquently explained: "This mighty swell of waters that giant forces press through the gate between Tierra del Fuego and the island, this crowding together of millions of tons of turbulent water, creates a sharp piling up of eddies and backwaters in which the largest ship can become unmanageable. Current fights swell, and the rocks wait with the cold sea snarling impatiently around them. It is not an ordinary ocean swell rolling on and on as one is accustomed to see. These waves rush perpendicular as if cast up by an invisible power, and fall to run again on the same spot—savage ship stoppers going nowhere but all 100 per cent against me." Piening asked himself: "What am I doing here?"

Yet the Strait of Le Maire, for all its dangers, was mere preliminary to the Horn itself, where colossal forces clashed because of two geographical anomalies: the huge unbroken expanse of ocean to the west and the relative narrowness of the Drake Passage, separating South America from Antarctica to the south. In the Southern Hemisphere below lat. 40°, the prevailing winds are westerly and gather strength as they make their way through the Indian Ocean and across the Pacific, building great sea swells that fling themselves against the vast, unyielding barrier of the Andes mountains coastal ranges. Because the Andes bring their continent farther south than any other large inhabited land mass, the crowding waves and winds are forced through the restricted opening between South America and Antarctica; Cape Squalls, with winds frequently up to 100 miles an hour, were known to windjammer sailors as Cape Horn

The tortured track of Captain Quick

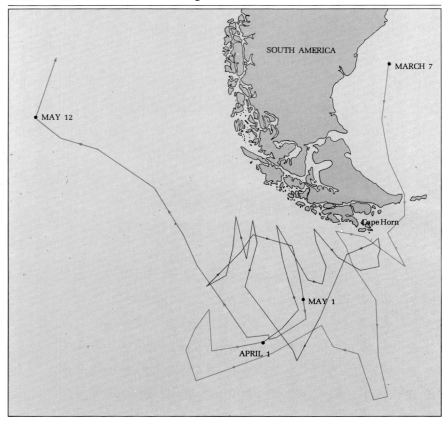

The agony of one of the most bitter bouts between a sailing vessel and "old Cape Stiff," as sailors called Cape Horn, can be seen in the tortuous track chart of the American windjammer Edward Sewall under the command of Captain Richard Quick. The passage took 67 days in the spring of 1914. Quick was twice blasted back to positions that he had passed weeks earlier; in the end he logged more than 5,000 miles to complete what in better weather would have been only a 1,500-mile voyage.

snorters, and the violent seas, the Cape Horn graybeards, surged as high as 60 feet. Moreover, the winds could change suddenly, and although they came screaming in from the west on an average of five days out of seven, they could turn right around and blow at the same strength from the east.

In its instructions to captains, the French windjammer firm of A. D. Bordes described the perils of Cape Horn weather in terms all the more dramatic for being stark: "It is nearly always very bad, even in summer. The winds blow almost continuously from the west, and although gales do not last so long in summer as in winter, they are more frequent and stronger. On the other hand, the winds are more variable in winter, the cold is more bitter and the hours of daylight are much reduced— lasting at most from nine to three—and there is mist and snow to make things even worse. In short, navigation is nowhere more difficult than in these waters."

Although Cape Horn is only a pinpoint, the expanse of sea dominated by its maelstrom weather conditions stretches several hundred miles both east and west of the Cape and all the way down to the Antarctic Circle. From lat. 50° S. in one ocean down around the Horn and back up to 50° in the other, the traditionally accepted boundaries of the region, is 1,000 miles, but with tacking, wearing and other course changes the usual distance covered by the windjammers was more like 1,500 miles. Going east, generally with the wind, often took little more than a week. But going west from 50° to 50° took from two to three weeks for the best of windjammers, and it took the French square-rigger *Cambronne* a full 92 days.

Against that, the fastest official time of five days and 14 hours, made by Captain Adolf Hauth in the Laeisz bark *Priwall* in 1938, near the end of the era of windjammers, beggared imagination. Hauth was the first to admit that "we were lucky, of course. It seemed as if this time the *Priwall* was determined to get past Cape Horn as if she never wanted to be taken there again."

There was, to be sure, a proper strategy—theoretical at best—for getting around the Horn to the west: it was to sail southwest against those bitter westerly blasts, taking every opportunity to "make westing," as sailors called their arduous westerly progress, and keep going until the ship was far enough along so that she could go on the port tack, heading northwest or north. There was also a chance that if a ship sailed far enough south, the wind might shift into the east for a blessed run west out of these terrible seas and into the tropical trades of the Pacific. The Cape Horn winds revolved clockwise around a low-pressure area. Thus, if the winds on the north side were rushing eastward, those on the south side would go the other way.

But too often the wind would not shift, not for days, sometimes not even for weeks, no matter which way a ship might go, no matter how tenaciously a crew might try to claw into the wind. On and on the wind would roar from the west or northwest. A ship suspended in its fury would make no westward progress at all but would be driven inexorably southeast toward the icebergs of Antarctica.

Set adrift from the antarctic ice shelf, bergs posed a special menace to windjammers. Some were incredibly huge, the world's largest masses in motion. The biggest ever recorded was a hook-shaped monster sighted in 1860 with one arm 60 miles long and the other 40. But such isolated islands of ice were not the trouble; the peril came from the endless fields of smaller bergs, virtual plains of ice that broke apart and rejoined unpredictably, in which a windjammer could suddenly be trapped. It might take days to sail clear—if the ship could get out at all. The French bark *Emilie Galline* in 1904 reported an incredible sight: an iceberg upon which an abandoned square-rigger was resting, fully out of the water. The *Emilie Galline* could not get close enough to make out her name or any other particulars. How she got there, what fate befell her crew, what subsequently happened to her are all lost to history. In 1906 the British *Monkbarns* was trapped in an ice field for 63 days; eventually the weather warmed and she was able to sail out. But the siege cost the life of her master, and many of her crew were nearly frozen to death by the time they escaped.

To avoid the ice fields, to make westing and clear the Horn, a captain had to be alert to every nuance of the wind. And when a change came, no matter how benumbed by his ordeal, he had to seize it instantly. The most successful Cape Horn masters were those who set as much canvas as the ship could stand, for only then could they immediately grasp any favorable shift in the wind and make distance to the west. That took courage—and stout ships.

Stories abound of the staying power of the windjammers. In 1905 the square-rigger *Deudraeth Castle* of the R. Thomas and Sons Company was so badly damaged in a Horn snorter that her master decided to abandon her. He and his crew were taken off by another windjammer that chanced by, but before he left the *Deudraeth Castle*, her captain had all her hatch covers flung open so that she would not remain afloat as a drifting menace to other ships. Six months later another windjammer in the area spotted the *Deudraeth Castle* still riding the Horn waves. A boarding party found her hull sound and her holds only partly filled with water. And, since the boarders neglected to scuttle her, for all anyone positively knows the *Deudraeth Castle* may be drifting yet somewhere in the remote ocean wastes.

Even more astounding evidence of a windjammer's incredible endurance was offered by the full-rigged ship *Dynomene*, under Captain W. S. Proctor, outward bound in 1907 from North Shields, England, to San

A bar sinister on the Pacific coast

One geographic name guaranteed to excite discussion in any fo'c's'le was that of the Columbia River Bar, guarding the channel leading to the grain docks at Portland, Oregon, about 94 miles upstream. For on this bar—alluvial deposits from the river's rush to the sea—numerous square-riggers of the "wheat fleet" came to grief at the turn of the century. "It is doubtful if any vessel was ever saved after being on the outer sands," warned the *Pacific Coast Pilot* in 1889.

There was no easy technique for a sailing ship to pass the bar, save behind the towline of a powerful steam tug with an expert pilot. Even in summer calms, swift tidal currents could sweep a vessel onto the shoals.

When the weather off the bar turned foul, the clash of the westerly swells of the Pacific with the great outpouring of fresh water from the Columbia generated an impassable crescent of surf. Throughout the storm-plagued winter months, scores of windjammers lay off the bar for as long as six weeks, awaiting a break in the weather and a tow.

So many parsimonious captains attempted to get across the bar on their own that cargo shipments in the early 1880s were seriously threatened. The angry citizens of Portland demanded safety measures. By 1885 construction had begun on the first 1,000 feet of a rock jetty that would extend seven miles and divert the tidal currents on the bar to make them scour a deep, straight channel through the sands.

Even so, the perils of running the inlet were never eliminated. Typical was the fate of the bark *Peter Iredale*. On the morning of October 25, 1906, she was suddenly swept onto the sands by a heavy southwest wind. According to one account, "the befuddled skipper found his ship amid a surging mass of breakers." The vessel crunched over the bar, and with the impact the mizzen top-hamper went crashing to the deck, which soon became "a welter of wreckage." By midday the *Peter Iredale* was a total loss—one of 96 vessels seized and destroyed in that one year by the guardian of the Columbia.

Her towline barely visible at extreme right, the French grain carrier Colonel de Villebois Mareuil passes across the perilous Columbia River Bar in 1912. The photograph was taken from the wheelhouse window of her escort tug.

Francisco with a cargo of pig iron, bricks and coke. The *Dynomene* had already rounded the Horn, looking for a change of wind that would allow her to turn northward, when she was seized by winds of hurricane force, stronger than 75 miles an hour. Since the barometer had been falling for several hours, the captain had been forewarned and consequently sail had been shortened down considerably, but when they struck, the violent winds quickly blew out all the *Dynomene*'s lower topsails with loud reports like thunderclaps. A number of braces, chain sheets and other rigging lines were carried away, and a topmast staysail was lost. Flying chain from the rigging smashed one sailor's hand that night, and a heavy sea that shipped over the forecastlehead broke bones as it carried two other men aft.

As the remaining crew members struggled to repair the damage, sparks flew from the clash of metal yards and masts. During the night the fore-topmast broke off and crushed a lifeboat. One of the yards plunged

through the forecastlehead into the crew's quarters. By a miracle, no one was hurt. The remaining yards swung madly around in the air with the ship's roll, threatening further havoc. Next, the main-topgallant and main-royal masts came plummeting to the deck, bringing with them all their yards and other gear. By morning the *Dynomene* was a shambles, most of her forward rigging a witch's web draped across the deck or hanging over the side.

The next day, the storm abated. The ship was hove to and all available hands went to work with chisels, hacksaws, mauls and any other tools they could find to cut and clear away the tangled gear. Makeshift sails were rigged to keep the vessel headed up into the wind. In the midst of the work, Captain Proctor was badly injured when a heavy piece of metal rigging came loose and struck him in the back. But he gamely refused to go below; every single man on board was vital if the *Dynomene* was to be saved.

As the *Dynomene* began limping toward the Falkland Islands for repairs, the weather again worsened. Soon the ship was being battered by another hurricane-like blow. A seaman fell from the rigging and was lost overboard. Such was the din of the tempest and the flapping of tattered sails that, when the mizzen-topgallant mast snapped and fell over the side of the ship, no one was able to hear it at all—though the men watched it go with fascination and horror. Now the top sections of all three masts were gone: the ship would have to be sailed with stump masts. A huge sea broke off the bowsprit, and another took away a massive teak and slate meat cask, weighing nearly a ton, that had been lashed tightly to the deck.

Again the *Dynomene* was hove to and the latest wreckage cleared away. Some hatches had been ripped open, and water was found in the

Bundled in glistening oilskins against the angry seas off Cape Horn, men of the Grace Harwar manage sober smiles during a 1929 passage with a cargo of grain from Australia to the British Isles. The combination of grueling work and ferocious elements prematurely leathered and lined seamen's faces; in the group above, only the carpenter (third from left) and the first mate (far right) are out of their teens.

hold. Yet another merciless storm struck, and the ship almost foundered on the Ildefonso Islets, an outcropping west of the Horn. A tremendous sea swept away the remaining lifeboats plus the fore-and-aft bridge, connecting the poop with the tops of the deckhouses; shortly thereafter, the wheel was smashed and the main compass and binnacle lost.

Somehow, no one remembered exactly how, the crew rigged more sails. A compass was slung in a hole carved in the top of the steward's sea chest to serve as a makeshift binnacle. It was lighted by a hurricane lamp mounted on a broomstick. The ship got under way again and headed east. Two weeks later, having been blown past the Falklands, she arrived off the River Plate and was towed into Montevideo. There the brave, battered *Dynomene* got new masts and rigging, had her decks patched up—and 13 weeks later set sail again, with a new captain and crew but the same pig iron, bricks and coke. This time she weathered the Horn without serious incident, and 92 days later she arrived in San Francisco, almost 11 months after leaving England.

Making westing against those awful head winds was by common consent the Horn's hardest challenge. But Cape Horn had something nasty for everybody. Eastbound windjammers always faced the threat of being pooped—overwhelmed from behind—by a massive graybeard while they were running before a heavy wind.

Rex Clements, on the *Arethusa* in the first decade of the 20th Century, described being hit by such a sea near the Horn. "Our progress," he said, "was slow, but not through time lost beating into the teeth of the wind. The furious gale kept ever on the quarter. The maindeck was a seething whirlpool, swept by endless tons of green water that made a dash for'ard a matter of life and death." The crew, drenched and exhausted from their efforts to control the ship, had gathered on the poop deck, watching, waiting and hoping that the *Arethusa*'s gear would hold. As they stood there, a tremendous breaker, much bigger than anything that had come before, built up astern. Until now the bark had ridden out the larger waves by lifting her stern at the last moment and allowing the surging water to pass under her. But this time the great breaker, foam-crested and steep-sided, advanced, rising higher and higher until it loomed over the taffrail.

"Hang on all!" cried the captain, and all hands struggled toward whatever rigging or deck gear seemed strong enough to hold them. With a thunderous roar the massive black wall of water crashed upon them. The water was head high, but somehow—though Clements remembered thinking his arms had been yanked out of their sockets—all the men hung on. The breaker swept past, moving forward to bury the rest of the ship. As the men regained their senses, the torrent enveloped and submerged the main deck. Only the forecastlehead was visible, an island in the ocean. The rest of the *Arethusa* was underwater. "My God," shouted the bosun, "she's gone!"

Not the *Arethusa*. "For a few seconds we lay stricken and a-swoon," Clements remembered later. "Another white-lipped monster was rolling up astern, but before it reached us the gallant old bark seemed to make a mighty effort. She quivered and labored heavily up, throw-

With white water surging around their legs, the crewmen of the four-masted bark Parma struggle (left) with a port-side winch in violent seas en route to Cape Horn from Australia in 1932. On the return voyage the Parma fought her way through heavy seas again; the picture above shows her main deck awash as a lone sailor clings to a handrail. The photographer was seaman-chronicler Alan Villiers.

ing water from her maindeck and lifting her streaming bows. As the roller swung down on us, her stern rose slowly to it, and it surged on and under, lifting the bark on its shoulders, spouting cataracts from every port." The *Arethusa* had survived—but at a cost. The breaker had swept away the wheelbox, destroyed the binnacle, splintered the cabin skylight and flooded the space below, littering it with fragments of wood and shards of glass. All unsecured gear on the poop deck was broken or washed away. The flying bridge over the main deck was smashed, and a lifeboat that had been mounted seven feet above the main deck was staved in.

"All hands were there, but more or less battered. Several of them were bleeding; the second mate was propping John Neilsen, white-faced and barely-conscious, up in the companion. The old mate lay under the mizzen rigging with his foot doubled up in a tangle of ropes, unable to rise. The steward, who was below in the cabin, was nearly drowned. The Horn had given us a rough baptism. We could not well have been nearer foundering than we were when that roller broke on us."

More than anything else, Cape Horn's storms were distinguished for their prolonged ferocity, striking for days without surcease, then resting briefly—and striking again. Few tales of journeys better exemplify that unrelenting fury than the miserable saga of the British Isles, the vessel in which apprentice William H. Jones had witnessed the windjammers' welcoming ceremony when he entered the port of Pisagua, Chile, in 1905. And well he might have appreciated that outpouring of friendship and assistance by the captains of the vessels anchored in port. For, according to Jones's later account of the ordeal, the British Isles had struggled for 71 days to round Cape Horn, during which she had taken what sailors called "a dusting" and experienced agonies almost beyond comprehension.

The British Isles was a three-masted, full-rigged steel ship, built in 1884 and thus a bit old by 1905. She was the largest vessel of her type ever launched from the Scottish shipyard of John Reid. Registered at 2,530 tons, she was 309 feet long and had a 105-foot main yard that carried a sail vast enough to challenge even the most efficient crew. "It was," said Jones, "as big as the wall of a church." The British Isles could make excellent speed running before the wind, but like most square-riggers, she did poorly when close-hauled. And that was a terrible deficiency when she was trying to beat against those screaming Cape Horn westerlies.

On this voyage, under Captain James Platt Barker, she was carrying some 3,600 tons of coal from Port Talbot, Wales, to Pisagua, Chile. Barker's crew of 20 seamen was a motley bunch, ranging in age from midteens to mid-fifties and representing 13 nationalities. Even before the British Isles left Port Talbot, seven members of her crew had deserted and had to be replaced.

The ship sailed on June 11 and enjoyed a fair-weather run across the Atlantic and down the coast of South America, arriving at the Cape on August 8. She even rounded the Horn in relatively good weather, and the captain began to hope for an easy passage. But soon after she had sailed by the headland, the barometer and the temperature dropped drastically, the strongest warning the region could offer for what it had in store. Sails were clewed up and furled by the time the storm hit. Young William Jones first saw the approaching gale as "a line of vivid whiteness" churning up "long oily hills of water." The squall, a Cape Horn snorter of hurricane force, slammed at the British Isles with sleet, hail and wind until her lee rail lay under the water. Spindrift froze on the rigging. Barker tried to keep sailing the British Isles generally to the southwest, but so great was the vessel's leeway that her wake streamed out at an angle of 60° to her keel, and by noon the next day she had been forced back east of the Cape.

At last, Barker ordered the ship hove to, with only a few sails set and the helm lashed down to keep her pointed up more or less to windward. Under this arrangement all she could do was drift inexorably southward, into the antarctic winter.

As the storm continued unabated day after day, the fo'c's'le and the apprentices' half deck were awash with several inches of icy water that surged back and forth with each roll of the ship. When working on deck, crewmen were drenched and their sea boots filled; aloft, their hands were fretted and cut by the frozen rigging. Most of them developed boils on their necks and wrists from the chafing of wet, salty oilskins.

Food rations were reduced, along with each man's daily allotment of fresh water—which was by now becoming salty, since the pump for the fresh-water tanks was in an open area abaft the mainmast, directly exposed to the sea water swirling about the main deck. Snow lay eight inches deep on the deckhouses. Weariness, hunger and thirst became each sailor's lot. "The scream of the wind," wrote Jones, "the crashing of seas, and the sickening lurches of the ship as she slid down the backs of the mountains of water, foretold that each watch would be a repetition of previous watches." On the sixth day of the storm, a seaman leaning over a yard to catch hold of a gasket being tossed up to him lost his balance in a sudden gust of wind and fell 40 feet into the water. Tremendous seas were running, and there was nothing anyone could do to save him. Soon another seaman, struck by a heavy sea breaking over the ship, suffered a deep head gash and had to be carried below, where the captain bandaged him as best he could. But the man's services were lost to the ship. Other crewmen were disabled by frostbite, and the fo'c's'le became a sick bay filled with groaning sailors.

The ship remained hove to and drifting. After almost 30 days, she had reached lat. 65° S., only 105 miles from the Antarctic Circle. Fragments of bergs, known as brash ice, rubbed against her sides, making "a curious and disconcerting growling noise." It grated on the men's nerves, and their resentments were fueled by the first mate, an able but surly man named Richard Evans. He held a master's certificate but had never been given a command. Disgruntled at having to serve as first mate under Barker, some 20 years his junior, Evans began to express his dislike of the ship and his fear that she could not make the Horn passage. At one point, egged on by Evans, a delegation of seamen demanded to know why Barker had not put about for the safety of Port Stanley in the Falkland Islands, only two or three days of downwind sailing to the north. The captain responded by shoving a revolver under their noses and shouting, "What damn fool on this ship thinks he knows better than I do about the course to set?"

Evans was not present, but the captain knew who the ringleader was. Barker rushed to the mate's cabin, shot the lock off the door and dragged the offending Evans into the messroom, where the crew was assembled. "Do you," he roared, "want to be logged for attempting to incite mutiny?" The white-faced Evans backed down, and that was the end of any trouble with the crew—but not with the elements.

On the 32nd day of the *British Isles*'s travail, the storm showed signs of slackening, and Barker decided that it might at last be possible to wear ship and change over to a port tack, heading in a northerly direction away from the antarctic ice. Some new sails were hauled aloft, bent to the yardarms and sheeted home, and there were cheers as the *British Isles* came around. But not for long. The barometer soon fell again, the wind rose and the ship was embroiled in yet another series of hurricane-force squalls.

At the height of the storm, the main-topgallant mast sheared off and

Shorn by a Cape Horn snorter of her mainmast and all but the stump of her mizzen, the 2,100-ton Wavertree lies forlornly at anchor in Port Stanley, Falkland Islands, in 1910. The falling masts gouged great holes in the deck and smashed her pumps and both lifeboats. Her crew, many of whom were injured, managed to keep the vessel afloat while she drifted to the safety of the Falklands.

Her decks alitter with storm wreckage, the dismasted Wavertree, judged beyond repair as a sailing ship, awaits a tow to South America. There she was put to lowly service as a storage hulk and sand dredge. But even waterfront laborers called her "the great sailing ship" — and perhaps the Fates were listening: in 1968 the Wavertree was acquired for New York's South Street Seaport Museum for restoration to her former glory.

came plunging down with all its yards and rigging. A crewman on lookout on the forecastlehead was swept away, never to be seen again. The ship's two lifeboats were lost, the main hatch cover was broken and its tarpaulin ripped. The side of the port fo'c's'le was staved in, and water surged around the bunks of the frostbite sufferers, who cursed and screamed in despair. "The only way of moving about on the poop-deck," said Jones, "was to crawl on our hands and knees. I have never seen anything to equal it in ferocity, in 50 years of sea experience since, and hope that I shall never see anything as severe again, either on sea or land."

With his ship half wrecked and the number of his effective crew down to six seamen and four apprentices, Barker decided that the time had come to give up the struggle. He would have to run for shelter after all. He ordered the first mate to square the yards and make for Port Stanley. Evans accepted the command, recalled Jones, with a slight smile.

More sails were sent aloft, and the *British Isles* made her way to the northeast, getting as far as Staten Island, outpost of the Strait of Le Maire. There, in the lee of the island, Barker paused. The *British Isles* was in the company of some 20 windjammers that had similarly sought refuge from the storm. Thousands of albatrosses flew among the anchored vessels or alighted on the water, white dots as far as the eye could see.

For three days the *British Isles* lay in the lee of Staten Island. Then a handsome German four-master, a P liner belonging to the Laeisz firm, swept through the bedraggled fleet, eliciting admiration and envy from all who saw her. Whether it was the sight of her or the fact that the wind had shifted around to the east, something made Barker change his mind: he would not give up. He would not go to the Falklands. He would set sail for the west and once again try to conquer the Horn.

By now it was late September, spring in the Southern Hemisphere and a time when the weather might be expected to soften. Instead the wind again rose to gale force, and the ship quickly found itself in the midst of a new tempest. With the *British Isles* rolling so violently that her masts described arcs of 60°, the crew once more went into the rigging to furl frozen sail, teetering on the icy footropes and, said Jones, "grunting, cursing and groaning as we labored in the darkness." After three hours of agonizing effort, they got in the mainsail and moved on to the equally cumbersome foresail. One man's fingers were crushed between the footrope and the yard: he recoiled in pain, lost his balance and plunged into the sea without chance of survival.

The storm continued for three days, then subsided; the wind shifted toward the southeast, allowing the battered *British Isles* to clear Cape Horn for the final time—52 days after she had first passed it. But there was one last crisis. In one of the early squalls, a seaman had been thrown into the scuppers, where his leg was beaten into pulp by a slamming wash-port door. The leg was now gangrenous and would have to be amputated. Barker got ready to perform the operation on a table in the starboard fo'c's'le—where the entire crew was now billeted.

The setting was dispiriting: poorly lighted, filled with smoke from a small wood stove, evil-smelling from the gangrene, and rolling and tumbling from the ship's movement in the still-heavy seas. Standing in inches-deep water and wielding the cook's knife and meat saw, Barker applied tourniquets to the thigh, cut away the diseased flesh, sawed the bone, cauterized the entire area with a red-hot poker and bound up the leg with cotton-wool dressings. The mutilated man faced many more days of pain, but he lived. And so did the woebegone *British Isles*. She finally limped into Pisagua after a 139-day passage. Her death toll was six men—three lost overboard and three others who later succumbed to injuries. It was, said William Jones, "a heavy price to pay for delivering 3,600 tons of black diamonds to Pisagua."

The number of windjammers lost to Cape Horn has never been calculated, nor has the number of men. The former might be in the hundreds, the latter certainly in the thousands. The Horn could kill swiftly, with a single murderous wave, or it could kill gradually, disabling ships and setting men adrift in their pitiful lifeboats on the vast uncaring sea. Those who endured shipwrecks off the Horn—and there were not many survivors—represented a sheer triumph of human spirit, for the odds were stacked against them. In July 1912 the British windjammer *Criccieth Castle* was disabled off the Horn while making a run from Peru to Antwerp with a cargo of guano. The ship was bashed by a heavy following sea that broke the rudderstock; the damaged sternpost caused a piece of steel plating to work loose, leaving a large hole into which water began to pour. The rudder was gone. The ship's pumps became clogged with guano and would not work; the powdered bird droppings on contact with water formed a gluey, stinking mass. Knowing that his ship was helpless and would soon sink, Captain Robert Thomas gave orders to abandon her.

With great difficulty, two boats were lowered. In the process the larger of the two was slammed against its davits, damaging its planks. The craft was nevertheless judged seaworthy, and into it with the captain went his wife, their four-year-old son and 14 others. A smaller boat carried the first mate and six crewmen. The two craft pulled away from the wallowing *Criccieth Castle* and set off toward the northeast, hoping eventually to reach the Falkland Islands, 180 miles away. Presently the wind increased and a hurricane was upon them. Night came, and both boats were tossed mercilessly about. The smaller boat disappeared and was never seen again. The captain's boat was alone. Snow, mixed with hail, was falling, and the bottom of the boat was awash. The cold was bitter: July is wintertime in the Southern Hemisphere.

In the morning, hopes soared as a large four-masted bark scudded past about a mile away. The lifeboat's occupants hoisted a blanket, waved clothing and yelled desperately. The bark sailed on and was gone.

Crushed by disappointment, spent from effort and numbed by cold, most of the crew subsided into a semiconscious stupor. They began to suffer delusions, insisting that they saw houses or roads, that the features of their boat mates had doubled in size or that they were back on the ship. Only Captain Thomas remained alert, manipulating the steering oar to keep the boat from being swamped. That evening three crewmen froze to death. Their bodies went overboard—but only after their oil-skins had been removed and wrapped around the captain's wife and son, who were lying in the bottom of the boat in the sloshing, freezing water.

Provisions consisted of two kegs of water, a fair supply of bread and a case of canned meat. But next day the bread was found to be ruined by sea water. The fresh water was already low, and the canned meat had been jettisoned to lighten the floundering, water-filled boat. With their hands swollen by frostbite, the survivors baled by holding a basin with their wrists. That day Captain Thomas was washed overboard. A crewman was able to grab the steering oar to keep the boat from broaching to, and the captain, arms flailing, made his way back to the craft. He hung on the gunwale. He could get no farther, and for a while no one could summon up the energy to help him. Finally, on weeping appeal from Mrs. Thomas, the men managed to get him aboard by clutching at his clothing with their teeth and arms. Later in the day another two crewmen died and were dropped over the side.

Two more days passed, the weather sometimes moderating, then blowing a gale. By the sixth morning the wind had diminished enough that a small sail could be set. Not long after that, land was sighted. Again their hopes were raised—and dashed, as the landfall turned out to be the uninhabited Beauchene Island. Food and water were almost gone. But the Falklands were only 40 miles north, and the survivors continued on. Toward the end of the day they managed to land on what turned out to be a part of the East Falklands. Staggering ashore, they stuffed snow into their mouths and gulped it down too fast, which made them sick. Next, they found a brackish pool nearby and drank from it; the salty water only made them sicker. Miserable and gagging, they spent the night huddled together in the snow to keep warm.

The following day Captain Thomas and a crewman set off to look for help. They returned several hours later to report that the island was uninhabited. A coasting vessel was sighted on the horizon, and they decided to make for her. A good offshore breeze was blowing, and they sailed well out to sea, only to lose their quarry. They tried to row back to shore but made no headway and so spent that night in the boat.

They were a haggard, pitiful group, their eyes bulging and tongues hanging out. Some foamed at the mouth. That night another seaman died. Just maneuvering his body out of the boat took nearly an hour.

Clearly the castaways could not last much longer. The next day the wind shifted, pushing them toward a rocky coastline, which spelled certain disaster. Captain Thomas tried setting another sail so that he could beat to windward and make for a distant headland, beyond which help might lie. Getting the second canvas rigged was painful work, but they got it up and headed toward the point. Hours later they rounded it. This time they were not disappointed. Ahead lay Port Stanley, the Falklands' largest settlement.

In the Port Stanley hospital two more crewmen died. The nine others survived, although some lost fingers or toes. The little boy at first seemed likely to lose both feet, but circulation eventually returned to them, and he emerged in good health. Captain Thomas needed crutches for a few months but soon was completely restored. As for Mrs. Thomas, she returned with her family to England, where, two months later, she gave birth to a baby girl, an unlikely survivor of the terrible voyage.

Captain Sea Devil of the "Seeadler"

o the British boarding officer, everything on the elderly windjammer seemed reasonably shipshape—as good as could be expected for a Norwegian tramp sailer that had recently been banged about by a fierce North Atlantic storm. It was Christmas Day, 1916, and the *Hero* had been forced at gunpoint by the British auxiliary cruiser *Avenger* to heave to for inspection in the open ocean 180 miles southeast of Iceland. This was of course wartime, and the British Navy had standing orders to stop and search all ships not immediately recognized as friendly. Now, after identifying himself with appropriate oaths as Captain Knudson of the 1,500-ton bark *Hero*, bound from Christiana, Norway, to Melbourne, Australia, the Norwegian skipper, in heavily accented English and between copious spits of chewing tobacco, invited the boarding officer below to examine the ship's papers.

The Norwegian appeared awash with holiday cheer. And that, reflected the British boarding officer, was a good thing, for the man looked to be a tough customer. He was a veritable giant, standing well over six feet, with a massive head, a walrus-thick neck, the shoulders and arms of a stevedore, and a voice that would have put a sea lion to shame.

The captain's saloon was in dreadful disarray, with papers strewn about, underwear (embroidered with the name Knudson) hanging to dry, and the air rank with the smell of kerosene smoke. "Excuse me, Mister Officer," said the captain, "but my stove is out of order. I could not know you gentlemen were giving me a visit today." Askew on a bulkhead was a photograph of a blonde, inscribed "Thy loving Josephine." And there, on the divan, lay Josephine herself, with a shawl tied around her head and an expression of anguish on her face.

"This is my wife, Mister Officer," said Knudson. "She has been having a bad go with the toothache." The British officer was sympathetic. "Sorry, madam, to intrude like this," he said, "but we must do our duty." "All right!" piped the stricken lady and lapsed back into silence.

As Knudson gathered up papers, he offered the visitor some refreshment. "Always give a British sailor a drink," he believed, "or a German sailor, or an American sailor, or any kind of sailor, for that matter." The boarding officer, clearly in the interest of international amity, accepted.

The papers and the logbook were damp and badly splotched—a result, as Knudson explained, of the storm through which the *Hero* had passed. As the inspecting officer began examining the documents, Knudson made small talk in Norwegian with his mate, noting at one point that he wished he owned a camel's-hair duffel coat like that of the British officer: "It would be fine to keep a fellow warm while up there north of the Arctic Circle." At that, the British officer remarked: "For rain and spray too." He had given no previous hint that he knew the language, and Knudson now gazed upon him in sudden and obvious respect. Finally, the examination was done and the British officer announced: "These papers are all in order, Captain." Upon leaving, he instructed Knudson to wait for a signal from the *Avenger* before proceeding.

That signal came in dramatic fashion. The *Avenger* got under way and steamed straight at the *Hero*, veering off only at the last moment. From her stern fluttered signal flags with the message "*Bon voyage*."

Haughty of mien and ablaze with medals, Count Felix von Luckner is the epitome of the World War I Imperial German Naval officer in this portrait memorializing his exploits as the commander of the windjammer-turned-commerce-raider Seeadler. The upper-lefthand corner bears an inscription from the artist, Emil Osterman, to his friend the "Sea Devil."

Bon voyage indeed. H.M.S. *Avenger* had let loose a scourge upon the oceans. The *Hero*'s real name was the *Seeadler*, or "Sea Eagle," and this innocent-looking old windjammer was in fact a German raider sent out with the personal blessing of Kaiser Wilhelm II to prey upon whatever vessels she could surprise and subdue. It was a mission of desperation: the Allied blockade of Germany was bottling up the warships of the Imperial Navy. Only German U-boats were able to slip through without coming into direct confrontation with Britain's Royal Navy, at that time the world's largest and most powerful fleet. But U-boats were limited in range because of their small fuel capacity. The German Navy high command realized that if armed surface raiders were to run the blockade and avoid detection by the enemy on the high seas, they would have to be camouflaged armed merchantmen—or auxiliary cruisers.

A few of these heavily armed converted freighters were dispatched through the blockade, disguised as ships of neutral nations, and began raiding the trade routes that were keeping the Allies supplied with food and matériel. But the Germans lacked coaling stations in the Atlantic and Pacific where their steam-powered auxiliary cruisers could refuel. One promising possibility for increasing Germany's depredations on the sea-lanes was to refit a fast and innocent-looking windjammer that would not need to refuel—and arm her with hidden weapons.

At first the idea was regarded as ridiculous by the German Admiralty, but its proponents would not give it up. As one Naval officer, Count Felix von Luckner, remarked to the Kaiser: "Well, Your Majesty, if our

While a seaman steadies the helm, Lieutenant Felix von Luckner barks orders into the engine-room telephone on the bridge of the cruiser Kaiserin Augusta in 1906. Although an able junior officer, Luckner often had a hard time of it during his first years in the Imperial German Navy. "I had been a common ordinary sailor," he wrote, "and this aroused a lot of antagonism in naval circles."

123

Admiralty says it's impossible and ridiculous, then I'm *sure* it *can* be done. For the British Admiralty will think it impossible also. They won't be on the lookout for anything so absurd as a raider disguised as a harmless old sailing ship.'' Thus the *Seeadler* was born.

Her master—the man who would assume the disguise of a Norwegian captain named Knudson—was Count Felix von Luckner. A lieutenant commander, Luckner possessed both experience in windjammers and a flair for dramatic action. He would come to be known as the Sea Devil.

Over the course of 224 days, the *Seeadler*, with Luckner at her helm, would prowl the South Atlantic and venture into the broad Pacific, a marauder under sail in an age of steam, dodging Allied squadrons, capturing and sinking thousands of tons of shipping. In some of Luckner's exploits incredible fact would outdo improbable fiction. And at the end, when World War I was over, this seafaring warrior would be respected and even admired by his British and French enemies.

But there is another aspect to Luckner's tale, one of broader import than simple derring-do. The cruise of the *Seeadler* was the last great naval duty of a ship under sail. As such, it came to symbolize a turning point in the history of the sea. The *Seeadler*—and her captain—were anachronisms in an age of ever-larger steam- and oil-powered dreadnoughts with their terrible 12-inch cannon and enormous shells that could penetrate a foot of armor at a range of 10 miles or more. True, the *Seeadler* was a raider, depending on guile for her prey. But as the last of her kind to make war, she sounded one final salute to the age of fighting sail, from Blake and Tromp to Nelson and Villeneuve.

Felix von Luckner was not the most sensitive of men. But he knew that he represented the end of an era. And he felt it deeply. ''One shouldn't ever have to sink a sailing ship,'' he said. ''They are the last survivors of the golden age at sea. The shipyards are not building many of them any more, and the day of the schooner, the bark, the clipper and the barkentine is fast passing. I have an old-time sailman's love for sailships. A steamer? Train the guns and light the fuses.''

Felix von Luckner was born to a family of Prussian warriors—mostly cavalrymen. His great-grandfather was a count who served as a cavalry officer in the army of Frederick the Great and later formed his own regiment of hussars, fighting as mercenaries for the French Revolutionary government—to such effect that he was named a marshal of France. Both Luckner's grandfather and his father rode for Germany as aristocratic hussar officers. It was to be expected that young Count Felix would follow in that glamorous service, which was considered—until World War I proved differently—to be the galloping breakthrough element of battle. Yet Felix, for reasons unaccountable even to himself, felt driven to the seas and to the great square-riggers that sailed them. But when he told his family of his desire to make a career at sea, his stiff-backed cavalryman father would not hear of it.

In 1894, at the age of 13, Luckner ran away from the family estate at Halle in Saxony, vowing never to return unless and until he became a full-fledged Naval officer. Wishing to avoid both the advantages and the possible harassments that might derive from his titled lineage, he assumed a new name, Phelax Luedige, from his mother's side of the family. For seven years he sailed in windjammers and other vessels all over the globe, learning the ways of the sea and encountering enough adventures to fill many lifetimes—which he would enjoy recounting with embellishments in later years. Nobody was ever quite certain where the facts ended and the embroidery began, for Luckner was a storyteller in the grand seafaring tradition. There are many examples.

His first ship was a Russian square-rigger, on which he served as a cabin boy. One day, in a South Atlantic blow, Luckner lost his grip and fell 90 feet from the rigging to the water. Floundering and flailing for his life, he caught hold of—or so he always said—the foot of an albatross, a huge bird with a wingspread of 10 feet, that had swept low over him. Despite the bird's vigorous efforts to peck him away, Luckner—again according to his account—held on until a rescue boat arrived.

He jumped ship in Australia to pursue a romance with a restaurateur's daughter. He was big for his age, and mature, and when the affair cooled he stayed in Australia doing odd jobs. He sold religious tracts for the Salvation Army, became a lighthouse helper (he was fired for making a pass at the keeper's daughter, an act that he insisted until the end of his days was no more than an innocent kiss), briefly joined a troupe of Hindu fakirs, worked as a kangaroo hunter and trained as a boxer.

Leaving Australia while still in his teens, he went on to several years of adventure on the high seas. He served on nearly a dozen ships in a multitude of capacities—including a brief spell as a cook—suffered all the hardships of the seafarer's log from scurvy to shipwreck, and saw the four corners of the earth. He later delighted in recounting how in Vancouver on one occasion he was arrested for prankishly stealing a fishing boat while his ship was tied up in port. On a voyage to Chile he was jailed again, this time for stealing pigs during a drunken shore leave. He was, he related, almost murdered by a psychopathic killer in Hawaii; he broke both legs at different times on voyages in the North Atlantic and the Caribbean and, when his ship sailed without him from Tampico, he served briefly as a presidential guard in Mexico City.

Among the many ships on which young Luckner sailed were two that made meaningful and lasting differences in his life. The first, a Norwegian square-rigger, he crewed from Havana to Australia and back to Liverpool. On board this vessel he became fluent in Norwegian.

The second windjammer was the *Pinmore*, a four-masted British bark built in 1882 and one of the best of her vintage. She was loaded with lumber, and on her Luckner made a horrible 285-day voyage from Vancouver to Liverpool, nearly dying of scurvy when the ship ran out of food and water while rounding Cape Horn. Awful as the voyage was, he forever afterward associated the *Pinmore* with the romance of his youth at sea. And in the end, she was to be the cause of a sad moment in his life.

In 1901, at age 20, Phelax Luedige at last returned to Germany. In a copy of the *Almanac de Gotha,* Europe's nobility roster, he found that his family had listed Count Felix von Luckner as missing. But he was not yet ready to go home—not until he had fulfilled his boyhood pledge to become a Naval officer. Continuing to hide his identity, he completed a navigation course, enrolled in the German merchant marine and became

Smiling demurely, with a delicate fan in hand, a German Navy man—dressed to impersonate the wife of a Norwegian skipper—stands good-naturedly beside Luckner as the Seeadler sets out from Bremerhaven. The costumed sailor played his part well when the ship was boarded and inspected by the British—so well, in fact, wrote Luckner, that the search officer "might have been talking to a court lady, instead of that rascal Schmidt."

a petty officer on the liner *Petropolis*, bound from Hamburg to South America. A year later he transferred to the German Naval reserve, undergoing further training and finally winning his officer's commission as a lieutenant. Now, at last, he could go home.

Dressed in full uniform, with gold braid, epaulets, sword sash and cocked hat, the young count knocked on the door of the family mansion in Halle and was ushered in by a maid. From another room he heard his father say, "Naval Lieutenant Felix von Luckner? There is no such man." Whereupon Felix entered and said, "Good morning, Father. I hope I have kept my word to wear the Emperor's uniform with honor."

It would have taken a hardhearted man not to have been impressed by such an entrance—and such a son. The elder Luckner greeted Lieutenant Felix with open arms, and from then on there was no question as to the course of the young man's career. Serving on various German steamships, he studied hard and earned his captain's papers, joining the regular Navy on February 3, 1912, for active duty. In due time Luckner won renown by rescuing five people from drowning—each on a separate occasion and each time refusing a medal for his feat. Such bravery won him wide notice in the press and fame as a hero, and he soon came to the attention of the Kaiser, whom he impressed and delighted in another way. From the Hindu fakirs in Australia, Luckner had learned some sleight of hand, and at a party attended by rulers and dignitaries, he impressed his emperor by wrapping an egg in a handkerchief, palming it, then producing it from the King of Italy's inside coat pocket. From then on, the Kaiser saw to it that Luckner got choice assignments—including service on board the cruiser *Panther* on an extended and pleasant inspection tour of German West African colonies.

When World War I broke out, Luckner commanded cruisers at the Battles of Heligoland and Jutland. At Jutland his vessel was sunk and he was rescued from the sea badly wounded. As soon as he had recovered, he was placed in charge of the *Seeadler* project.

It was only natural that Lieutenant Commander Felix von Luckner should be her captain. He was an officer of imagination and proven courage. He spoke impeccable Norwegian—and the flag of neutral Norway would be an ideal cover for a disguised German raider. Above all else, Luckner was one of the few young officers of the Imperial Navy with extensive windjammer experience.

The Germans had acquired the *Seeadler* by a fluke. She had been built in Scotland in 1888 and, as the *Pass of Balmaha*, was known for her speed. Shortly before the War, her British owners had sold her to an American firm, and in 1916 she was bound for Archangel, Russia, with a load of cotton when a British cruiser stopped her for inspection. Though the United States was neutral, the cruiser's commander ordered her taken, and put a prize crew aboard. After replacing the American flag with the Union Jack, the prize crew headed for Scapa Flow.

But they never got close to their goal. The very next morning a German submarine surfaced and captured the *Pass of Balmaha* with her cargo of cotton. The British prize crew was superseded by a German one, and the ship was sent into the German base of Cuxhaven. During the next year, as the British blockade tightened further around them, German authorities converted the *Pass of Balmaha* into a camouflaged raider.

The architects of the renamed *Seeadler*—chief among them Luckner—achieved one of maritime history's most memorable disguises *(pages 136-143)*. From keel to top deck, Luckner recalled, the three-master became "a mystery ship of trick panels and trick doors." In addition to quarters for an extra-large 64-man crew, there were hidden accommodations for 400 prisoners. Luckner insisted that these quarters be as comfortable as possible, equipped with proper bunks and toilet facilities and stocked with books and magazines.

"If I took any prisoners," he said later, "I wanted them to feel as though they were my guests." It was a gesture as shrewd as it was gentlemanly; well-fed, well-treated prisoners were less likely to cause trouble—or to give the alarm when the *Seeadler* was approaching an intended victim.

Crew members were chosen for their knowledge of sailing ships as well as their coolness and proficiency in combat. Many of them spoke fluent Norwegian. One sailor, a slender and beardless youth named Schmidt, was outfitted with a blond wig and a dress, and rehearsed for the role of the skipper's wife, Josephine. The fake female served Luckner's notion of the English as men who were innately—and distractibly—courteous toward women.

Luckner himself forsook the narrow-stem pipe he ordinarily clenched in his great jaw and endlessly practiced chewing and spitting tobacco, a habit for which Norwegian sailors were notorious. Moreover, as Luckner said, "A chew of tobacco gives you time to think. If somebody asks you an embarrassing question, you can roll the quid around in your mouth, pucker up your lips slowly, and spit deliberately and elegantly."

By the time such quaint training exercises were completed, German intelligence had found a Norwegian windjammer that looked much like the *Seeadler* and whose identity she could assume. She was the *Maleta*, now unloading in Copenhagen, and scheduled to take on a new cargo at Christiana, sailing at about the time the *Seeadler* would be ready.

It would naturally help to have her logbook—clearly a job for Phelax Luedige, who (by his own accounts) chanced to turn up at dockside in Copenhagen, where he got a job as a longshoreman. He observed the habits of the ship's lone watchman and, one night when the crew had all gone ashore, stole aboard the *Maleta*, went forward, cut her mooring lines almost all the way through, then returned aft and waited. The tide ebbed, lowering the ship and tightening the hawsers until they snapped with a loud noise, which awakened the watchman and sent him scurrying to the bow. In the darkness Luckner crept below and found the logbook under the captain's mattress. He shoved it under his belt, raced up the gangplank to the wharf and vanished into the night.

By mid-November, 1916, the bogus *Maleta*, with her forged papers, fake cargo, concealed heavy armament, play-acting crew and amiable captain, complete with spouse, was ready to break out of Bremerhaven through the British blockade. Her departure was timed for the day after the real *Maleta* was scheduled to leave Denmark. But at the very last moment, Imperial Navy headquarters ordered her to wait. The U-boat *Deutschland* was heading home to Germany after a much-publicized

Assuming their disguises as neutral Norwegians crewmen of the German raider Seeadler gather on deck atop a false cargo of timber before setting out to run the British blockade in 1916. The elaborate charade included phony names and caches of fake personal possessions. "Every man had his rôle," explained Luckner. "Each man had to fix in his mind a whole new past life, according to the life of the sailor whose rôle he was to play."

Mustered for a formal photograph, the Seeadler's crewmen proudly wear their German uniforms. Both officers and men were hand-picked for the daring mission by Luckner himself. "I tried to read these men's souls," he was later to declare dramatically, "in order to discover in them the qualities of courage and endurance that would be needed."

visit to the then-neutral United States. The German submarine's presence in local waters was therefore known to the British. The enemy would without question be doubly vigilant, and the high command did not want to expose the *Seeadler* unduly. But by the time, three weeks later, that Luckner finally received his sailing orders, the real *Maleta* was long gone. Luckner's ship would need a new faked identity. One other Norwegian square-rigger listed in Lloyd's Register fitted the circumstances: the *Carmoe*. But after forging her name to the *Maleta's* papers, Luckner learned that the real *Carmoe* had been seized by the British and taken into port for examination of her cargo. In desperation, Luckner picked the first name that came to mind: *Hero*.

The new name would now have to be entered on all the ship's papers and in the logbook. But the logbook from the *Maleta* would not take further tampering; any more erasures would make the forging obvious. Luckner had a brain storm. He summoned the ship's carpenter and bosun. "Get an ax and smash all the portholes, windows, everything," he ordered. "And drench everything with sea water." Furniture was broken, railings bashed. Water was poured onto all the carpeting, into the bunks and sea chests—and especially over the ship's papers. "Now repair everything," said Luckner. "Nail it all up, the way you would at sea." The patched-up vessel, looking like a ship that had just emerged from an Atlantic blow, her documents understandably water-stained and blotched, set sail and headed into action.

Into action—and into a true hurricane, which remarkably proved to be her salvation. Running the blockade required getting past a vast mine field. Luckner knew the mines were planted several feet below the surface to inflict maximum damage on a deep-draft steamer or warship. But sailing ships drew less water and one that was heeled over under full canvas drew very little. So he cracked on sail and used the wind to lean his ship almost onto her beam-ends and pass safely over the mines. After that, getting by the British cruiser *Avenger* two days later was fool's play.

The *Avenger* had scarcely signaled her *bon voyage* salute that Christmas Day in 1916 when Captain Felix von Luckner began to show his own—if not his ship's—true colors. Out went the nauseous tobacco plug and back came the incongruously dainty pipe. Off came a face-hiding foul-weather hat and on, at a jaunty angle above a prominent brow, went a peaked skipper's cap. Dropped from his vocabulary were the Norwegian skipper's coarse obscenities, only to be replaced by a euphemistic "by Joe," always uttered in English. The crew donned their German Navy uniforms, the Norwegian flag was temporarily replaced with the Imperial flag, and beer, schnapps and wine flowed freely as the officers and crew prepared for a belated Christmas celebration.

Once the festivities were over, the *Seeadler's* crew jettisoned the fake cargo of Norwegian lumber. The two 4.2-inch guns were uncrated and positioned behind the bulwarks on the port and starboard bows. The *Seeadler* was now ready for battle. But light cosmetics of disguise were retained to enable her to approach intended victims as closely as possible; these included tarpaulins over the guns, canvas name flaps that could be dropped down over the *Seeadler's* own name at bow and tran-

Under full sail and flying her battle ensign, the Seeadler surges down an ocean swell to close with another victim in this 1920s painting by German artist Christopher Rave. Depicting the attack on the French bark Antonin in 1917, the work is based on a snapshot made by the skipper of the hapless vessel, who, according to Luckner, "staggered back with a dramatic gesture that only a Frenchman can achieve when he saw the German flag at our masthead."

som, and canvas Norwegian flags that could be unrolled on her sides.

Luckner's orders from the high command were to seek out and destroy only sailing ships. A windjammer capturing a steamer was ludicrous. Yet on the morning of January 9, 1917, when a lookout shouted, "Smoke on the port quarter," Luckner did not hesitate to ignore his mandate. "By Joe," he once said, "I could sink a steamer and laugh as she takes her last dive." Now, for his first victim, he intended to take this one.

As the vessel approached, Luckner hoisted a signal asking for chronometer time. It was a reasonable request, for an aging windjammer rarely had a good chronometer or a wireless, and customarily checked the ship's time with that of other vessels. The steamer slowed momentarily, replied that she understood and maneuvered to windward so that the *Seeadler* could heave to for the chronometer time.

At an order from Luckner, the *Seeadler* then raised the German ensign and unmasked her hidden 4.2-inch port gun. The steamer turned to run but Luckner fired across her bow. After three more shots over her bow, stern and smokestack, her astonished captain hove to and rowed over to the *Seeadler*. "You fooled me bloody well," the steamer's master told Luckner. His crew was disembarked and transferred to the *Seeadler*, where they were led down into the prisoners' quarters. At nightfall the detonation of an explosive charge placed in the steamer's hold announced the end of the British freighter *Gladys Royale*, carrying coal from Cardiff to Buenos Aires. She was only the first of many victims.

The next day, the *Seeadler*'s lookout again spied smoke on the horizon. With strong following winds, Luckner put the windjammer over to head across the enemy bow and again raised a signal asking for chronometer time. But this steamer, unlike the *Gladys Royale*, did not respond. In fact, she continued steering straight toward the *Seeadler*, in flagrant disregard of the maritime rule giving sail the right of way.

Veering off just in time to avoid a collision, Luckner hoisted the red and black German ensign, showed the *Seeadler*'s guns and fired a few warning shots. When the steamer turned to flee, Luckner fired pointblank into the hull and smokestack. That was all it took. The steamer, another British freighter, named the *Lundy Island*, surrendered and her crew was brought on board to join that of the *Gladys Royale*.

It turned out that the British captain had been suspicious of the *Seeadler* from the start. Some sixth sense had told him that the big windjammer flying Norwegian colors was not all she seemed. So he had tried to bull his way past, and for a personal as well as a military reason. Some months before, he had lost another ship to a German armed merchantman. He had been released, however, after promising not to engage in further war activity. Now he was terrified that he might be hanged from a yardarm for failing to keep his pledge.

Indeed, once on board the *Seeadler*, the British captain found himself face-to-face with a German medical officer who had served on the auxiliary cruiser that had sunk his previous command—and who knew of his promise. But the always-chivalrous Luckner assured the anxious skipper that he need not fear for his neck. As he dispatched a crew to scuttle the *Lundy Island* and her cargo of coal bound from Madagascar to France, Luckner merely sent the freighter's captain down to the prisoners' quarters, where he soon became engaged with the captain of the *Gladys Royale* in an intense rivalry at checkers.

The prisoners were confined to their secret quarters only during battle situations, and otherwise had the run of the ship—able to amuse themselves with games or to join in work details, for which they were paid the wages they were accustomed to receive from their own shipowners.

For 10 days no vessels were sighted. At last, on January 21, sail was spotted on the horizon. Luckner had posted a $50 reward plus a bottle of champagne to the man who sighted the next ship. And British prisoners, including the captains, were clinging to the rigging alongside German seamen, enthusiastically scanning the sea with binoculars and spyglasses. "Never," recalled Luckner, "had a ship such a lookout."

The vessel turned out to be the French square-rigger *Charles Gounod*, bound from South Africa to Bordeaux with a cargo of grain. She was soon run down, captured and sunk, but only after the captain and crew had been taken aboard the *Seeadler*—along with many cases of red wine.

Over the next three weeks, three more windjammers, a Canadian, a Frenchman and an Italian, were captured and sunk, and only the French vessel gave any trouble. She was the four-masted bark *Antonin*, a smart-looking ship and a fast one, to judge by the way she was sailing. This was just the sort of challenge Luckner most enjoyed. Firmly refusing to use his auxiliary engines, he determined to take the *Antonin* by outsailing her. At first, the *Seeadler* gained little in her sail-against-sail pursuit. But when the vessels moved into a squall, the French captain routinely took in his royals and upper topgallants; Luckner drove the *Seeadler* under full sail. "The captain of the *Antonin* thought we were quite mad," Luckner recalled. "Gallants and royals up during a storm—he had never seen such a thing in all his days at sea. The sight was so funny that he wanted a picture of it." Close enough now to see the photos being taken, Luckner ordered his crew to fire one of the *Seeadler*'s machine guns.

"First he was startled," Luckner said of the French skipper, "then he glared: 'What did these lunatics mean?'" Next, according to Luckner, the French captain "began to roar at us in the most profane French. When a Frenchman swears," said Luckner, "you can hear it far off." Yes indeed—apparently even over the howl of a squall.

After the *Antonin* had surrendered, her captain and crew were welcomed into the *Seeadler*'s growing company of prisoners. "But first," recalled Luckner, "we seized that Kodak and roll of film, by Joe."

It was all highly exciting and quite within the international rules of naval warfare. But amid the adventure there came one occasion when Felix von Luckner was torn between the memories of his past and the demands of his present. On February 19, 1917, the *Seeadler* ran down and captured the *Pinmore*, the stately four-masted British bark that had once been home to the young runaway Phelax Luedige.

After the *Pinmore*'s crew was transferred to the *Seeadler*, Luckner rowed alone to the old windjammer and went aboard. He walked the decks he had walked so many years before. The big ship, rolling gently in the swells, was quiet. Luckner went into the fo'c's'le and found his old bunk. Still on the ceiling above it was a hook he had himself placed to hold a can under a leak. He walked to the stern rail, on which he had once

On the Seeadler's deck, captured Allied captains join Felix von Luckner (second from left) in sampling cognac and champagne plundered from the British steamer Horngarth. "I had my own ideas as to how our prisoners should be treated," said Luckner, who entertained his "visitors" with concerts and offered them cards as well as books and phonograph records in English and French.

carved his name. There, dimly visible, it remained: Phelax Luedige.

Returning to the Seeadler, Luckner decided—probably out of a mixture of nostalgia and necessity—to sail aboard the Pinmore one more time. He later recounted his bold plan: "Having been now a considerable time out, I checked our stores and found that we were becoming very short of certain articles, chiefly tobacco, cigarettes, fruit and vegetables. I decided, as we were only about one hundred miles from Rio de Janeiro, to sail the Pinmore into that port myself." Since most of the Pinmore's crew had been Norwegian, it was possible for Luckner's fake Norwegians to impersonate them on this risky venture. "As I had discovered that the Pinmore had no agents in Rio," Luckner recalled, "I conceived that with fair luck I should win through safely."

His arm in a sling to cover his inability to forge the real captain's signature, he sailed into neutral Rio in March 1917. The Pinmore was greeted by the usual tugs and customs officials. The charade presented to the British officers of the blockade cruiser Avenger was repeated for the Brazilian harbor officials, and the ship's papers were pronounced to be in order. Once towed to an anchorage, Luckner went ashore personally to arrange for the needed supplies.

Returning quickly to the wharf, Luckner's good fortune helped him again. He met a British military officer who informed the Sea Devil that as soon as his cruiser, the *Glasgow*, completed her coaling stop, she was off to join a sister ship, the *Amethyst*, in the hunt for a German raider that had been reported about 100 miles west of Trinidad.

Forewarned of the strong enemy presence and not eager to run the risk of further conversation—or of encountering Brazilian friends of the *Pinmore*'s real captain—Luckner hurried back aboard the commandeered windjammer. Harbor launches soon arrived with the stores he had ordered, including 350 pounds of tobacco, 20,000 cigarettes and 50 boxes of cigars. Receiving routine customs clearance, the *Pinmore* slipped quietly out of Rio and three days later rendezvoused with the *Seeadler*.

Transferring the fresh stores to his own vessel, Luckner braced himself for a personal ordeal. After clearing the *Pinmore* of valuable equipment and dispatching a demolitions team, the count went below to his own cabin on the *Seeadler* and shut the door. There, in solitude, he waited for the sound of the dull explosions that would send the *Pinmore*, and an important fragment of his early career, to the bottom.

But the *Seeadler*'s career was only beginning. On March 5 a French windjammer, the *Dupleix*, was easily taken and her captain, when brought aboard the *Seeadler*, seemed in high spirits: he apparently thought it all some sort of joke. Only when Luckner ushered him below to the saloon, where portraits of the Kaiser and assorted German war heroes were hung, did the Frenchman's amusement vanish. "We are lost," he wailed. The prisoner was not only desolate but embarrassed. Back in Valparaiso, it seemed, two fellow French masters had warned him of enemy raiders and advised him to cable his owners for instructions. He had foolishly ignored their counsel—and look what had happened. "What were the names of your friends' ships?" asked Luckner. The *Antonin* and the *Rochefoucauld*, said the captain. Luckner turned and spoke quietly in German to an orderly: "Bring up captains five and nine." When the two entered the room, the latest arrival recognized them instantly as the friends (the *Rochefoucauld*, along with a Canadian bark named the *British Yeoman*, had been taken without incident a week or so before) who had evidently failed to follow their own sage advice. "Eh," he cried, "All of France is here!"

One morning the following week a lookout sighted a large British steamer, and Luckner went in pursuit. Her name was the *Horngarth*, and on closer look she proved to be equipped not only with a wireless but with a 5-inch gun as well. Luckner began with his standard ploy, a request for chronometer time. No reply. The German then ignited a set of chemical pans atop his deckhouses, sending up licks of flame and billows of smoke; he also hoisted a distress signal. Fire at sea was something that no ship could ignore, and the *Horngarth* approached the windjammer and hove to. But both the wireless and the gun still had to be neutralized. Luckner decided to provide a distraction: he cut off the smoke and flames but ordered his "wife," the blond Josephine, clodhoppers hidden by a long gown, to sashay back and forth on deck.

While the *Horngarth*'s master and men gathered at the rail to ogle her, Luckner ran up the German flag, showed his guns and began shooting at

The French windjammer *Charles Gounod* sinks bow first into the Atlantic depths, the third vessel to fall to Luckner. Watching from the *Seeadler*, the French crewmen clutched their caps to their breasts, and their captain wept while Luckner, in mock sadness—because "I had to sink my favorite composer"—hummed a lament from Gounod's opera *Faust*.

A 30,000-mile trail of havoc in the name of the fatherland

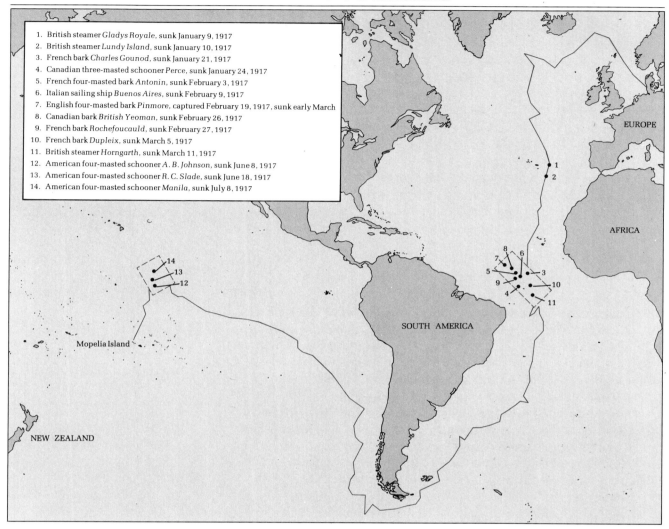

1. British steamer *Gladys Royale*, sunk January 9, 1917
2. British steamer *Lundy Island*, sunk January 10, 1917
3. French bark *Charles Gounod*, sunk January 21, 1917
4. Canadian three-masted schooner *Perce*, sunk January 24, 1917
5. French four-masted bark *Antonin*, sunk February 3, 1917
6. Italian sailing ship *Buenos Aires*, sunk February 9, 1917
7. English four-masted bark *Pinmore*, captured February 19, 1917, sunk early March
8. Canadian bark *British Yeoman*, sunk February 26, 1917
9. French bark *Rochefoucauld*, sunk February 27, 1917
10. French bark *Dupleix*, sunk March 5, 1917
11. British steamer *Horngarth*, sunk March 11, 1917
12. American four-masted schooner *A. B. Johnson*, sunk June 8, 1917
13. American four-masted schooner *R. C. Slade*, sunk June 18, 1917
14. American four-masted schooner *Manila*, sunk July 8, 1917

On her seven-month cruise through the Atlantic and Pacific in 1917, Count Felix von Luckner's Seeadler captured and scuttled 14 Allied ships (indicated by heavy dots) before she met her own violent death at Mopelia in the Society Islands. Though she traveled 30,000 miles, the hunting was profitable only in the sea-lanes off northeastern Brazil between South America and Africa, where she took nine ships in less than two months. The cruise in the Pacific was uneventful except for the sinking of three American trading schooners.

the wireless shack. A direct hit demolished it. As an added effect, the *Seeadler*'s crew had rigged a fake cannon, made out of an old smoke-stack, that emitted a resounding report and belched a great cloud of smoke—and they now "fired" it at the *Horngarth*. The British captain began yelling orders to man the 5-inch gun. But Luckner, in yet another bluff, had placed three men with megaphones aloft. On cue they shout-ed, in unison and in clear English: "Torpedoes clear!" The response from the steamer's bridge was immediate: "No torpedoes, for God's sake, no torpedoes!" The *Horngarth* surrendered, but there was one sad result of Luckner's victory: one of the *Horngarth*'s officers had been hit by stray metal during the firing on the wireless. He died on board the *Seeadler* and was buried with honors, the Union Jack draped over his body.

The *Seeadler* had so many successes that before long her prisoner area held 262 officers and men. Luckner was anxious to clear the captives out so that he would have room for more. On March 21, as he headed south toward the Horn, he came upon a square-rigger that suited his purpose. She was the French bark *Cambronne*. Her master exhibited the predictable despair at the prospect of losing his ship, then was astonished to hear that she would not be sunk after all. Instead, she would carry the prisoners to Rio de Janeiro. Luckner needed a captain whom he could trust to keep the Seeadler's secret as long as possible, and so he appointed the senior captain present—the ex-master of the Pinmore, whom he respected—to the post, extracting a promise from him not to communicate with any other ship before reaching Rio. Part of the Cambronne's nitrate cargo was dumped into the sea, her topmasts were cut off to slow her down, and the prisoners were placed on board.

As the Cambronne moved away toward Rio, Luckner sailed north until he was out of sight and then turned abruptly south. When the Cambronne prisoners arrived in Rio and passed the word that Luckner had charts of the Horn region, a number of British cruisers and auxiliaries were dispatched to the area. But the Seeadler was not to be found.

Racing south after sending his prisoners to Brazil, Luckner managed to clear Cape Horn before the British Navy could rally to intercept him. Nearing the equator in mid-Pacific two months later, the Seeadler sank three large four-masted American trading schooners, the A. B. Johnson, the R. C. Slade and the Manila. Compared with the Atlantic prey, these were slim pickings—and Luckner was now low on supplies. Beriberi and scurvy had broken out among prisoners and crew, and he had to find a safe harbor where he could replenish food and water.

On July 31, 1917, the Seeadler anchored off Mopelia, a lush but sparsely inhabited atoll in the Society Islands. That night the captain, crew and prisoners went ashore to feast on turtle soup, broiled lobster, gull's-egg omelet and coconuts. Two days later disaster struck the Seeadler.

There are two versions of the story. To his dying day, Luckner insisted that a huge tidal wave swept over the horizon and hurled the Seeadler to her doom against a reef; by a miracle, all those aboard survived the crushing impact. In this, Luckner was loyally supported by his crew.

But the American prisoners swore to a different story. They insisted that Luckner had anchored foolishly close to the reef surrounding Mopelia. On the day of the accident, he was ashore with most of his crew enjoying a picnic, while the American prisoners and a few Germans remained on board performing maintenance chores. It was flat calm but a powerful current was running, and the Seeadler, apparently dragging her anchor, began to drift toward the reefs. Before anyone could do anything about it, the ship crunched into the coral and was hard aground, her keel broken in five places.

The truth seems to lie with the Americans. Luckner, authentic hero though he was, apparently invented the tidal wave to hide his horrible embarrassment at losing his ship in a preventable accident. Weather records kept by the French on the nearby island of Tahiti make no mention of a tidal wave in the month of August 1917.

In any case, after the disaster, the crew salvaged what they could from the wrecked Seeadler and built a village of huts with ship's timbers, sailcloth and palm leaves. Their prisoners, all Americans, christened the streets Broadway, Pennsylvania Avenue and the Bowery. There was still plenty of wine left from the capture of the Charles Gounod—plus quanti-

Her keel broken when she went aground on a coral reef in the Society Islands, the *Seeadler* sends forth clouds of black smoke after Luckner and his crew stripped her of provisions and set her ablaze. "We were castaways in one of the loneliest reaches of the South Pacific," wrote the captain. Yet the crew retained its indomitable spirit, and he could add: "Everything lost, but we stand like an oak."

ties of cognac and champagne from the *Horngarth*—and ample supplies of tobacco. But after three weeks, boredom set in for the adventurers.

"The monotony was beginning to get on our nerves," Luckner recalled. So he and five crewmen decided to make a valiant effort to escape from their island exile. They rigged a salvaged lifeboat with a mast and sails, stocked her with provisions and weapons—one machine gun, carbines, pistols, hand grenades, bombs and 1,000 rounds of ammunition—and set out to capture the first island trading ship they came upon.

Heading eastward toward the Cook Islands and the Fijis, the tiny craft was buffeted by strong winds and heavy seas. Bailing constantly, tormented by the sun and the chafing of their salt-spray soaked clothes, and subsisting on a diet of hardtack and salted bacon, Luckner and his men endured the ordeal for 28 days. At last, they fetched up on Wakaya in the Fijis after a spectacular voyage of 2,300 miles from Mopelia. There they were confronted by a British officer and four soldiers from a local garrison. Luckner considered resisting with his superior weapons, but in the end decided that it would lead to pointless killing. The Germans surrendered and their mission was over. They were shipped off to internment in New Zealand until the War was over.

All told, during his dramatic seven-month cruise of commerce-raiding 30,000 miles down through the South Atlantic and across the Pacific, Luckner—the Sea Devil of the *Seeadler*—had surprised and captured 14 vessels belonging to five Allied nations. Three of them had been steamers and 11 had been sailing vessels, mostly windjammers like his own. In the aggregate, as one observer wrote, this daring German nobleman had "scuttled $25 million worth of shipping, and wrought incalculable damage by delaying hundreds of cargo vessels from venturing out of port." Yet, with it all, Luckner's proudest boast to the day he died at the ripe old age of 85 in 1966 was that he and the *Seeadler* had caused only one death—that of the British officer on board the *Horngarth*, accidentally killed by the flying metal of a shellburst.

As for the windjammers themselves, their twilight as commerce carriers deepened rapidly during the War. Large numbers—there is no record of exactly how many—of French, British, Italian and American windjammers carrying grain, oil and war matériel to Europe and the British Isles were sunk in the North Atlantic by German U-boats. Between 1914 and 1919 the famed French firm of A. D. Bordes lost almost half its fleet, 22 big windjammers out of a total of 46. Other shipowners in the French city of Nantes on the Bay of Biscay bemoaned the loss of 36 windjammers to enemy action. For the Germans, the War was even more disastrous. It caught large numbers of windjammers in Allied or pro-Allied ports, and there they stayed for long years, the vessels useless, rusting and pathetic, the skippers and crews bored and miserable. In Valparaiso, Chile, alone 25 big German windjammers were interned, and though they went home with full loads of nitrates after the Armistice, their day was clearly done.

The War, as wars so often do, had brought great advances in the technology of ship design and steam propulsion. Economical oil was taking over from coal in steamship boiler rooms. Owners, captains and crewmen turned to steam in ever-increasing numbers—until only a few diehards remained to work and love the tall, white-winged ships.

A masterpiece of disguise for a weapon of war

She was as innocent as she was beautiful—the American windjammer *Pass of Balmaha*—until the German Imperial Navy seized her in 1916 and turned her into a sinister weapon of war, an auxiliary cruiser whose role was to surprise and destroy enemy shipping.

Her conversion was a masterpiece of disguise. Beautiful she remained, and innocent she looked, but beneath her sleek lines and towering canvas, this splendid three-masted full-rigger, now renamed the *Seeadler*, or "Sea Eagle," carried claws as sharp as those of her namesake. In a Bremerhaven shipyard, workers installed secret panels hiding passageways from which heavily armed German Navy men could suddenly rush on deck. Tucked in her bows were two 4.2-inch cannon, ready to blast unsuspecting enemy ships out of the water. Below her water line, her keel was rebuilt to hold a diesel engine that would allow her to pursue victims when the wind was down. Two motor launches were put aboard, ready to be swung over the side with boarding parties. Because she was expected to take large numbers of prisoners, secret quarters were built for them in the ship's hold—secret in case the *Seeadler* was inspected by a more powerful enemy warship.

To disguise her as a neutral Norwegian windjammer, Norwegian chronometers, barometers, thermometers and other hardware were installed. The captain, Count Felix von Luckner, and 16 of the 64 carefully chosen crewmen were fluent in Norwegian. One of them, Seaman First Class Heinrich Hinz, described their costume: "The crew dressed like Norwegian seamen with Träsko wooden shoes, thick woolen Icelander sweaters and blue shipmen's caps, and carried Norwegian tobacco, Skraa chewing tobacco and above all Norwegian identity papers. Many all of a sudden got 'fiancées' in Norway who wrote letters full of longing. We let our beards grow and took Norwegian names."

When the *Seeadler* emerged from dry dock and slipped out to sea, she was a killer on the prowl in the costume of a classic tall ship. Many skippers would be lured to their doom—to watch their own ships destroyed and vital cargoes lost. And before her deadly voyage ended in the far Pacific, the *Seeadler* would become a legend.

Disguised even during her conversion in a Bremerhaven dry dock, the Seeadler assumes the name Walter and poses as a training ship being outfitted for cadets. Workers at her stern fasten a four-bladed propeller to a shaft already installed through the keel to the ship's afterhold, where an engine bed had been prepared. Other workmen (far left) uncrate a donkey boiler engine that will provide power to help the crew work winches and to raise and lower the ship's hidden guns and motorboats. Under the gaze of armed Navy guards, workers replace her rigging and repaint her hull while onlookers watch, unaware of her mission.

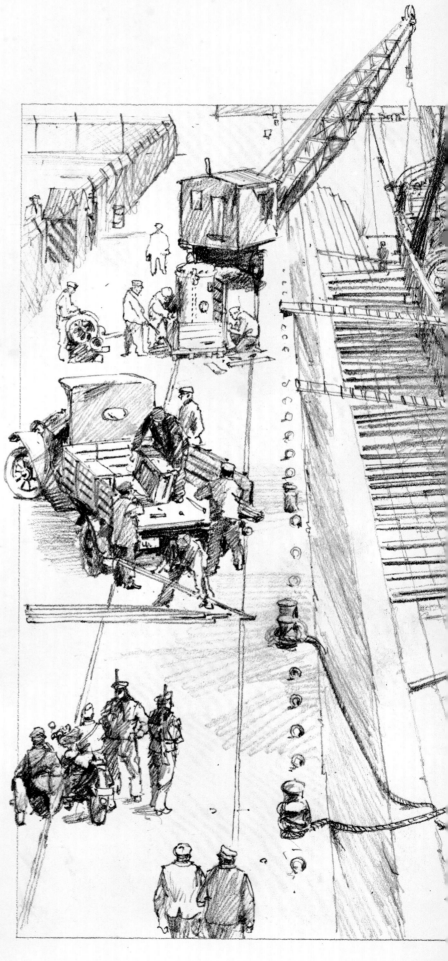

Engineers and workmen lower a 1,000-horsepower diesel into the hull of the Seeadler. The diesel, invented 20 years earlier by Munich-educated Rudolph Diesel, was built in Copenhagen. With it the Seeadler could attack ships even in calm seas.

A carpenter installs secret panels in the captain's quarters to allow armed crewmen to enter from hidden compartments in the ship's rebuilt hold. Invisible in the baroque woodwork, the secret door enabled Luckner to call in German marines to overwhelm any enemy warship's officers who might board the Seeadler, demand to inspect her papers and then become suspicious of her disguise.

To accommodate the Seeadler's prisoners, metalworkers build canvas pipe berths into the new false bulkheads of the ship's hold. Identical quarters and berths were installed for the ship's armed crew. On a tripod in the center foreground is a pipe vise; a threader for the pipe ends lies amid debris below.

Anchoring off the German coast, the Seeadler makes a secret rendezvous with a tugboat towing two lighters carrying Norwegian lumber — each plank stamped with the markings of a Norse lumbermill. This false cargo was destined for no foreign port but was meant to complete the raider's careful disguise.

Hauling the planks aboard with a boom hoist, the Seeadler's crew — dressed as Norse seamen — stack the lumber over the ship's hatches. By blocking access except by secret passages, the Germans planned to keep search parties, should the ship be halted at sea, from finding the quarters for combat crew and prisoners.

Dropping her disguise, the Seeadler reveals herself to her first victim, the British freighter Gladys Royale, bound for South America. With the canvas tarp now off the port 4.2-inch gun, crewmen—all wearing Imperial Navy uniforms—rush to uncrate and load shells. Eager for the kill, the Seeadler's gun crew aims and fires over the steamer. The Gladys Royale raised the Union Jack and turned to flee, but three more shots from the Seeadler and the British captain surrendered. A German prize crew, mustering with rifles and machine guns at left, boarded the abandoned freighter, placed charges in her bilge and scuttled her.

Chapter 6

Trustee of a vanishing way of life

Ever a soft touch for a square-rigger,
Captain Gustaf Erikson stops for a chuckle
at two model windjammers displayed
on the hatch cover of one of his own barks,
the Ponape. A canny businessman and
a master mariner to boot, Erikson owned
and operated some 20 sailing ships
in the 1920s and 1930s—the last great
deepwater sailing fleet in history.

The lordly steel windjammers, more than a dozen of them, all flying the Finnish ensign with its field of white quartered by a sky-blue cross, rode comfortably at anchor in the pine-girt harbor, their topmasts and yards towering over the simple frame houses near the water's edge. The serenity of the scene was broken only by a little wood-burning tugboat named *Johanna*, which bore the letters "GE" on her funnel and went skittering from ship to ship like a water bug on a lily pond.

Perched atop the tug's wheelhouse and gesticulating with a cigar butt was a stumpy, square-faced old man who from time to time disembarked to limp aboard one of the windjammers, which he scoured with his gaze, poking into the holds and even struggling aloft to inspect the yards. "I see to it that they are free of rust," the old man had once said, "that the gear is good and the rigging sound, that the masts and yards will carry their sail round the Horn and anywhere else that I send them."

The tiny, out-of-the-way harbor was at Mariehamn, in the Åland Islands, between Sweden and Finland, and by this time, in the 1930s, it had become the windjammer capital of the world. The stumpy old man was Captain Gustaf Erikson, owner of the initials on the tug—and of the last major fleet of windjammers to sail the globe.

For almost two decades Erikson had valiantly struggled for survival with a score of secondhand windjammers. There was no chance of victory over the long haul; time was inexorably against him, and defeat and extinction of the windjammers could be the only outcome. Yet stubbornly and singlehandedly Erikson tried to stave off the inevitable. "I love those ships," he said. "When I go, they go, but while I stay, they stay."

World War I and its aftermath meant ruin to deepwater merchant sail. Not only were many sailing ships sunk; their markets were gone. Synthetic nitrates, developed in response to wartime demand, deprived the windjammers of their most valuable cargo, natural nitrates from Chile. And full postwar use of the Panama Canal enabled steamers to shortcut sailers on vital trade routes, notably from the west coasts of North and South America to the American east coast and Europe.

As advancing technology made steam more and more practical, the great maritime powers abandoned sail. By 1923 Lloyd's Register listed only 28 British-owned sailing vessels of 1,000 tons or more. The last British Cape Horn cargo carrier met her doom when the *Garthpool*, launched in 1892, was wrecked on the Cape Verde Islands in 1929. In France the estuaries of the port cities were filled with windjammers

being dismantled. So many were anchored in a canal near the Loire River that the place was called "the Cemetery." The famed firm of A. D. Bordes sold its last ship, the *Atlantique*, in 1926 and went out of business.

In the United States there were several belated attempts to put the great tall ships to successful postwar use. But most failed. One of these involved German windjammers that had been seized in U.S. ports in 1917 and, in an outbreak of romantic whimsy, given Indian names, reputedly by Mrs. Woodrow Wilson herself; thus the *Dalbek* became the *Monongahela*, the *Steinbek* was now the *Arapahoe*, and an especially strong, fast ship, the *Kurt*, was renamed *Moshulu*, meaning "fearless." They were set to carrying lumber from the Pacific Northwest to Australia, but the American owner, who had bought them cheap from the U.S. government, had problems contracting cargo and eventually went bankrupt. His best ship, the *Moshulu*, was sold in 1935 for a beggar's asking of $12,000—to Gustaf Erikson of the Åland Islands.

As the losers of the War, the Germans saw their magnificent merchant fleet, both sail and steam, virtually wiped out. The Treaty of Versailles required that Germany cede to the Allies all her merchant shipping of 1,600 gross tons or more—a level that included every windjammer.

In the early 1920s the once-great Laeisz firm of Hamburg made a valiant effort to recover, buying back several of its old ships and trying to make a go of it in the waning Chilean nitrate trade. They even built a new vessel: the *Padua*, a four-masted bark of 320 feet and 3,064 tons, and

Big Cape Horners of Gustaf Erikson's fleet line the rocky periphery of the little port town of Mariehamn in this 1935 painting by a Swedish artist. Trailing a plume of smoke is Erikson's tiny tug Johanna, which he used to travel about the anchorage, constantly checking to make sure that everything was shipshape on board his beloved windjammers.

launched it in 1926—the last true Cape Horner to leave the ways. But not even Laeisz could cope with the economics of the time. By the early 1930s the company had scrapped or sold all but two of its square-riggers. The proud owner of five former P liners was Gustaf Erikson.

With 18 windjammers, Gustaf Erikson was the last owner of a major deepwater sailing fleet. And indeed, the final years of the windjammers can be told only in terms of Gustaf Erikson; of his people, the seafarers of the Åland Islands; and of his ships, especially his most beloved *Herzogin Cecilie*, the great windjammer that took the measure of the British steamer on a blowy October morning in 1934 in the South Atlantic.

He was a true Ålander, a native in spirit as in sinew of the glacier-carved cluster of some 6,000 islands and rocky islets in the narrow passage between the Baltic Sea and the Gulf of Bothnia. Historically and ethnically, in their language and their manners the Ålanders were Swedish, and their ancestors were among the Vikings who had roamed the world's waterways more than 1,000 years before.

But in the winter of 1809, Russian troops attacked across the ice and captured Åland, the group's largest island. In the subsequent Treaty of Frederikshamn, Sweden ceded the entire Åland archipelago—along with Finland—to the Czar, under whose flag the islands remained until the Bolshevik takeover in 1917. Then, although the nearly 30,000 Ålanders voted by a referendum for a return to Sweden, the League of

Nations granted them self-government, under the sovereignty of Finland, which had proclaimed its independence from Russia in December 1917. There they remained, not quite Finnish and not quite Swedish.

Throughout it all, the Ålanders were faithful to their two natural endowments: the gently rolling farmland just inshore and the surrounding sea. Because the farmland was dispersed over so many small islands, a farmer often had to reach his outlying fields by boat. Gradually a pioneer form of cooperative enterprise grew up. Groups of farmers would take shares in building a schooner or brig from native timber. Each shareholding family contributed a man or a boy toward the crew, and the little ships ranged the Baltic, selling Åland produce.

The Ålanders saw in deep-sea windjammers a way to extend their horizons beyond the Baltic and North Sea. They built some of their own, and they purchased others—always secondhand and at bargain prices— as owners elsewhere began to discard sail in favor of steam.

They were a thrifty people. When an Åland shipowner named Robert Mattson bought the full-rigger *Thomasina Mclellan* from the British, he shortened her name to *Thomasina*, supposedly to save on cabling costs. And it became an Åland rule of thumb that the profits of the first three or four years of trading by one vessel, carefully salted away, would be enough to buy another. On that theory, the citizens of a village like Vårdö, with a population of under 1,000, before World War I could buy and operate 21 square-riggers.

The Ålanders also had a sheltered, virtually tideless deepwater harbor at Mariehamn, located at the southern tip of Åland Island. With an onshore breeze, a ship could sail right up to her moorings by the town. The spick-and-span little town naturally reflected its residents' chief interest. A government-supported navigation academy certified masters and mates; a number of leading citizens had windjammer figureheads in their gardens; and models of sailing ships hung as decorations and inspiration from the ceilings of the churches. It was far from being the least of Mariehamn's advantages that the town could at a moment's notice supply seamen, from captain to cabin boy, for a ship in need.

Gustaf Erikson was heir to all this. The son of a sailing man, he was a ship's boy at nine and at 13 a cook. Although there is no record that he ever attended the Mariehamn school maintained by the authorities for sea cooks, he did have an intense, and often aggressive, lifelong interest in ship-style food. Years later, as a successful shipowner visiting London on business at least once a year, he always stayed in a modest hotel, where he got evident enjoyment out of complaining that the chef could not prepare a proper mariner's pea soup—with chunks of salt pork.

Once, the crew members of a bark about to sail from an Erikson shipyard laid aft to petition the captain to do something to vary the ever-present strömming soup, a hearty concoction of Baltic herring that ranked high on Erikson's bill of fare. Instead of finding the master, who might have heard them out quietly, they were confronted by Erikson, who happened to be on board and who delivered a furious oration on the dangers of insubordination and the virtues of strömming soup.

When he was 19, Erikson became the captain of a short-haul Baltic and

Stars of the North: the Alaska Packers

Long after most shipping companies had given up sail for steam, here and there an outfit found some unlikely use for the stately old windjammers. One such venture was that of the San Francisco-based Alaska Packers' Association, a fishing concern that made high profits by specializing in salmon.

About 1901 the Packers began to buy up the sturdy old Cape Horners that other firms were discarding. For the next 30-odd years, every April, after a winter's idling *(bottom, right)*, the ships went gliding northward through the Golden Gate Bridge, bound for the salmon-filled waters off Alaska.

The ships of the Packers' Star Line— so called for the names bestowed on the ships: *Star of England, Star of Scotland, Star of Alaska* and more than a dozen other "stars"—were specially equipped for the job. Every vessel carried a whole work force of its own— which might comprise as many as 200 Chinese laborers—and 5,000 tons of supplies, all they would need for six months to come: box staves, tin plate, solder, traps, seines, boats and rice.

On arrival in Alaska after a month's passage of some 2,500 miles, the crew turned fishermen and put off in boats; the laborers went to work, making cans, building crates, and readying themselves to split, clean and pack the fish as fast as the fishermen could haul in their catch.

Throughout the summer the windjammers lay at anchor, taking on the cargo *(top, right)* as it was ready. In September they headed back to San Francisco, carrying as much as 120 million pounds of salmon, canned, crated and ready for dispersal all over the world—a mass-production venture made possible by the last American square-riggers on the sea.

At Naknek, Alaska, three sailors hoist crated salmon aboard a Star Line vessel.

Waiting for next year's salmon run, the Star of India idles in San Francisco Bay.

North Sea trader of the sort known as "onkers" because of the "onk-urr, onk-urr" racket made by their windmill deck pumps. After two years of that, he decided to broaden his horizons, and gave up his coastal master's ticket to ship out as a mate on a deep-sea vessel. By age 30 he was a master again, this time on long-voyage Åland barks that took him to all parts of the globe. But a nasty fall from the rigging left him permanently crippled in his right leg. His seafaring days were at an end, and in 1913 Gustaf Erikson left the sea to set himself up as a shipowner.

His first vessel, bought for less than $10,000, was an old 1,500-ton bark, the Tjerimai. Her previous owners had found her uneconomical. Erikson made her pay from the beginning. He bought her stores himself, never purchasing too much or too little. He subjected her to a stem-to-stern inspection when she came into port and personally supervised all repairs; he was a master sailmaker and cut her sails himself. He fixed her freight rates and arranged her charters. In short, he was a one-man shipping company. Then he applied the old Åland formula and parlayed the Tjerimai's profits into the purchase of more ships.

During World War I, Åland's ships were still flying the Russian flag, and in consequence they suffered at the hands of the Germans. At the outset of hostilities, 14 of the ships were taken in German ports, and two

Sitting beneath a metal can that has been pierced to spill its collected rain water and then slung from a lifeboat, a crewman on the deck of the Herzogin Cecilie takes a welcome shower while his shipmates wait their turns. Because the duration of every voyage was uncertain, a windjammer's supply of fresh water was strictly rationed—except after a tropical storm. Then, recalled one Cape Horn captain, "Everything and everyone aboard revels in soap and water."

more were rounded up off the coast soon afterward. On one awful day in 1917, three of the finest Åland ships were sunk. Erikson's *Borrowdale* and his *Margareta* were both sent to the bottom by German submarines. Yet while many of his fellow shipowners were driven under by losses, Erikson prospered because of good luck and good management. He lost no other ships to raiders or submarines and took advantage of booming wartime freight rates. The freight rate from Argentina's River Plate to the United Kingdom, for example, rose from 12 shillings a ton in 1914 to 65 shillings in 1915 and 146 shillings in 1916.

When the inevitable postwar windjammer decline arrived, Gustaf Erikson was ready with cash on hand to buy secondhand ships at scrap prices. Among his acquisitions was the British-built *Lawhill*, a four-masted steel bark that under Erikson came to be known as "Lucky *Lawhill*" because of her freedom from mishap and her remarkable fortune in finding good freights. On a 1921 voyage to Argentina, at a time when few ships were getting cargoes, she picked up a cargo in Buenos Aires that paid Erikson an incredible single-voyage profit of $200,000.

The great key to Erikson's success lay in his being the soul of frugality. Known to his Åland friends as "Gusta," he earned the nickname "Pjutte Gusta"—roughly translated as "Stingy Gusta"—from his crewmen, who commemorated his thriftiness with a ditty:

Pjutta Gusta, this is truth, Hoards every little copper coin,
Buying schooners and barks—Old, rotten Noah's arks.

A penny pincher he was, but for high purpose—and therein lay his anguish. He was sentimental about his ships, but he could not afford to manage them sentimentally. If he did, steam competition and diminished cargoes would surely take their toll—and, he said, "If I lose my ships, I lose everything." And so Stingy Gusta skimped and scrounged and cut costs with vast ingenuity.

With only three helpers, one of them a typist, he ran his great fleet out of a shedlike office, from which his booming voice could be heard plainly on Mariehamn's main street. Once, he asked a candidate for a mate's berth if he preferred any one ship over the others. The man replied that he liked them all but would rather not serve on either the *Lawhill* or the *Grace Harwar*, since they were old, hard driven and past their prime. Gusta was outraged. "All my ships are first class!" he roared. "The best of cordage, the best of canvas, the best of paint. What utter nonsense!"

Gusta's claim to the contrary, he diligently hoarded supplies. In the 1930s a crewman going through the sail locker of an Erikson ship came across a sail whose German markings indicated it had been made before 1914. Damaged sails were patched and used as "tropical rags" in place of the newer, heavier storm canvas required by North and South Atlantic gales. Such savings were crucial to Erikson's survival. He operated on a narrow margin and once calculated that he would be doing well to clear an average of $3,200 a year on each of his vessels. Sails were expensive and the windjammers went through them at an appalling rate. Canvas cost Erikson between $1,200 and $2,000 per ship in good years and much more in bad times—such as when the *Herzogin Cecilie* lost 19 sails in 30 hours during a blow off England's Scilly Isles.

On the rare occasions when disaster befell an Erikson ship, everything possible was salvaged. When the bark *Hougomont* was fatally dismasted off Australia's southern coast in 1932, the *Herzogin Cecilie* soon lay alongside to take all salvageable items back to Mariehamn. Before long the *Hougomont*'s charthouse was fitted to the *Penang*'s poop, her wheelhouse appeared on the *Killoran*—and her figurehead showed up as an ornament in Gusta's garden. (Erikson's first act after purchasing the *Herzogin Cecilie* herself was to rip out the fittings in the quarters provided for some 60 cadets during the ship's days as a training vessel. The area was converted into stowage space for sails, and everything marketable was sold—including the companionway.)

It was only natural that Pjutte Gusta should pay meager wages: $60 to $80 a month for his masters and only eight dollars for an ordinary seaman—considerably less than steamship operators were paying. But he told his men—and he may even have believed it—not to worry because the opportunities for windjammers were so great. All those smoke-belching steamships would soon gobble up the world's fuel supplies—and then another great day for windjammers would dawn.

The Åland Islanders may have smiled inwardly at such talk. Yet in those islands, wages were not the only thing in life. And there was such

Stevedores slide sacks of grain into a hatch on board the Grace Harwar at a jetty in Wallaroo, Australia, in 1929. A number of sacks would inevitably burst, so the crew lined the holds with old sails and burlap to keep loose grain from falling into the bilge and clogging the pumps. It took more than 60,000 sacks to fill the hold of a typical 3,000-ton windjammer.

gallantry involved in the old fellow's fight to save the windjammer that he never lacked for captains and crews.

Erikson even worked out a system whereby he was actually paid by men working for him. The Finnish government required that all prospective ships' officers, including those headed for steam, have apprentice training in sail. Erikson was only too delighted to provide this training: he charged each apprentice $200 a year for the privilege of working on an Erikson windjammer and, as wages, returned two dollars a month—which came to $24 a year. Sometimes the payers outnumbered the payees. In 1932, for example, the *Archibald Russell* carried a crew of 24 men before the mast. Of these, only four were receiving wages.

In the dying days of the windjammers, Gustaf Erikson discovered that tidy profits were offered by paying passengers of romantic or nostalgic tendency. For about $400 each, the passengers spent some seven months at sea on a working windjammer. Before sailing, they signed articles as members of the ship's company and, though they were not required to crew, if anyone wished to perform deck chores Gustaf Erikson would have been the last to stand in the way. One of his vessels, the *L'Avenir*, between commercial trips once made a pleasure cruise in the Baltic, complete with orchestra, dance floor, bar and a swimming pool. The *Herzogin Cecilie*, in 1932, made space for four passengers on a regular voyage. And since one of them was a woman, the courtly Gustaf Erikson, penny pincher though he was, went so far as to employ a stewardess.

But passengers were of course no more than an attractive sideline. Erikson managed to prolong the life of the windjammer by his unerring choice of the only remaining market in which sail still possessed clear advantages over steam. This was the Australian grain trade. And although Erikson certainly did not invent it, he used it to far greater advantage than anyone else. South Australia was one of the world's great wheat-growing areas. Yet shallow, reef-infested waters and primitive facilities that often required weeks for loading made the Australian trade both hazardous and uneconomical for deep-draft, high-overhead steamers. Grain, moreover, offered an ideal cargo for windjammers. It was relatively light, easy to handle and, once harvested, almost imperishable. It was, therefore, little affected by the average 120-day passage of the windjammer from Australia to Europe. Finally, the schedules of the producers and the carriers dovetailed perfectly: the windjammers could make only one round passage a year to and from Australia, but then the wheat growers could reap only one annual harvest.

For Erikson and a few smaller shipowners, the benefits of the grain trade were inscribed in black ink. In the 1930s, for example, windjammers usually profited at least five dollars a ton on their wheat cargoes. A square-rigger carrying 3,500 tons of grain could thus net $17,500 on a single voyage. Still, agriculture is at all times and in all places the chanciest sort of business. For Erikson to send his entire fleet in ballast to Australia, a total of some 200,000 unremunerative sailing miles, in hopes that full cargoes would be waiting required a plunger's courage. That Gustaf Erikson possessed in abundance.

In the early 1930s, as Erikson settled fully into the grain trade, a sort of yearlong fleet ritual evolved. In late autumn, after repair and refitting in the Mariehamn harbor, the tall ships would set forth. They usually stopped at Copenhagen to take on supplies and adjust compasses, a complex and laborious process requiring several tugs to pull the vessel around to precisely determined headings. The departure from Copenhagen was described by an admiring British observer: "The mates of each ship kept on deck eyeing the weather, and as towards evening the wind slid round to a more favourable quarter their knuckles rattled on their skippers' doors and announced the news.

"The blowing of whistles set off a ruffle of activity in each ship. The clonk and rattle of anchor chains coming in started the gulls mewing in alarm, and their clamour mingled with the shouts of mates and crews. Figures scuttered along yards, frantically loosing gaskets, and the wings of the big square-sails unfolded in drooping points as the clews came out. The jibs fluttered a moment, the helmsman brought the wheel over, the tops'ls filled their bellies with a sigh, trembling as they tautened, and the ships' long lean bodies began to slide through the water, gathering speed swiftly as sail after sail flowered aloft."

Ahead, some 15,000 miles and half a world away on the southern coast of Australia, lay the Great Australian Bight, its bleak coastline extending for 1,600 miles and marked by such forbidding place names as Cape Arid, False Bay and Anxious Bay. At the extreme eastern end of the bight, between Cape Spencer and Cape Catastrophe (named for a boat wreck in which eight lives were lost), a tide-torn finger of water reaches 180 miles into the Australian back country. The inlet is Spencer Gulf, and there, at ramshackle villages called Port Augusta, Port Germein and Port Pirie, the last of the windjammers lay alongside dilapidated piers to load grain at the height of the harvest, during the Christmas season.

It was a tedious process. Port Germein, for example, had a cargo jetty that extended more than a mile, but only at its farthest end was the water deep enough to permit a windjammer—and then only one at a time—to load. In 1936 Erikson's *Killoran* awaited her turn for 40 days. But Port Germein was luxury in comparison with Port Broughton and Port Victoria, where the square-riggers had to anchor well offshore—sometimes several miles—while farm hands loaded the grain bag by bag onto ketches and schooners for ferrying to the windjammers.

By springtime the job was done and the ships headed homeward, usually by way of Falmouth in southwest England or Queenstown in southern Ireland, for orders about where to unload before returning to Mariehamn. On Erikson's vessels it was customary to spend the last half of the voyage from Australia engaged in overhaul and spring-cleaning, readying the ships for the stem-to-stern inspection they were certain to get from the old man at the instant of their arrival in Mariehamn.

The meticulous attention Erikson paid to the condition of his ships was especially necessary to him as an uninsured shipowner: disrepair had a cumulative effect, almost sure to lead to major damage, the cost of which would fall upon Erikson alone. He once said of his ships: "I cannot afford to have them insured. If I had to pay the rates the underwriters ask, I would have to give them up, every one." Yet by painstaking care—combined, to be sure, with a large measure of benign fortune— Erikson and his fleet wrote a remarkable record for safe passages. During

Crewmen aboard the Parma, homeward bound from Australia to Falmouth in the early 1930s, overhaul the shroud screws and seizings of the standing rigging while the ship's cook cleans the deck boards leading to the galley. No matter how old a storm-battered windjammer might be, tradition demanded that the crew spruce her up before she entered port and came under the owner's critical eye.

his more than 30 years as a shipowner, a venture attended by risk along every mile of the way, Erikson lost only three ships to the elements. Yet each mishap contributed to the eventual doom of the windjammer.

No agency on earth could have prevented the disaster that befell the *Hougomont* on April 21, 1932. That she even survived to be cannibalized for other ships in the fleet testifies to the skill and tenacity of her crew. The vessel was overtaken in the Great Australian Bight by a vast black cloud bank that unleashed cyclonic winds of up to 100 miles an hour. After she had spent nearly 12 hours fighting the storm, all that was left of her top-hamper were the stumps of her foremast, mizzenmast and lower jigger mast. The *Hougomont* remained afloat and was eventually towed into port, but the repair estimate, nearly $13,000, was exorbitant, and she was finally stripped and scuttled to form a breakwater for the Stenhouse Bay jetty in Spencer Gulf. Though distressing, the accident could have been worse for Erikson: sailing in ballast, the *Hougomont* had carried no cargo for which the uninsured shipowner could be called to account.

Three months later, in July 1932, the four-masted bark *Melbourne* became Erikson's second casualty. The ship had a lurid past. In 1908, sailing as the *Austrasia* out of Liverpool, she had arrived in Rio with her sails in tatters, her master in irons, and both mates suffering bullet wounds. The master was later tried for shooting the second mate and was adjudged insane. Now, as Erikson's *Melbourne*, she was near Fastnet Light off Queenstown when she was rammed by a tanker. In his agitated efforts to save the ship, the *Melbourne*'s master fell from the poop to the main deck, breaking both legs. The first and third mates tried to save him—and were drowned with him when the ship sank. Once again Erikson escaped financial ruin: the tanker had been clearly at fault, and the owners made reparations for the *Melbourne* and her cargo of grain.

And then, shortly before 4 a.m. on April 25, 1936, the *Herzogin Cecilie*, the flagship of Erikson's fleet and for 15 years his greatest joy, went aground only 49 miles out of Falmouth.

The *Herzogin Cecilie* was built in 1902 at the then-enormous cost of more than $200,000 as a cadet training ship for the North German Lloyd steamship company, whose specifications required a fast, smart, four-masted steel bark with generous cargo capacity and accommodations befitting future officers of Imperial Germany's merchant marine. She was named after Duchess (*Herzogin* in German) Cecilie of Mecklenburg, who later became the crown princess of Germany, and she was indeed a princess—even a queen in her own right. She was in fact the epitome of those square-rigged sailing ships described by an enraptured English chronicler as "the stateliest and most beautiful creations for which the mind of man has ever been responsible in the whole of his history."

For 12 years she carried cargo—and cadets—under the Imperial German flag, a cynosure wherever she appeared. Then, for six gloomy years, she gathered rust as a wartime intern in Coquimbo, Chile. After the War, under Versailles's retributive terms, the *Herzogin Cecilie* was allotted to the French—who were getting out of sail as fast as they possibly could. They had no thought but to sell her for whatever she would bring.

Late in 1921 Gustaf Erikson of Mariehamn dispatched his most trusted captain, Ruben de Cloux, an Ålander of Belgian descent, to Marseilles to inspect the former Laeisz four-master *Passat,* now also in French hands, which Erikson had heard was for sale. On the way, de Cloux stopped in the Belgian port city of Ostend and saw the *Herzogin Cecilie* at anchor there. He looked no further. (In fact, not for another decade did the *Passat* enter Erikson's fleet.) Upon his captain's advice, Erikson bought the *Herzogin Cecilie* for the astonishing price of $20,000.

Erikson adored her. He made her his flagship. He posed proudly for photographs on her deck. He invited friends aboard her for *kakfests,* or cake parties. She was allowed to retain her gleaming white hull; black paint, more durable, less vulnerable to stain and therefore cheaper over the long run, covered other Erikson vessels.

Erikson entrusted the *Herzogin Cecilie* to his best captain, de Cloux himself, a powerfully built man with huge, gnarled hands, a careful sailor with a wizard's instinct for wind. In 1929, when de Cloux retired, his place on the *Herzogin Cecilie* was taken by his mate, Matthias Sven Eriksson, then only 25, another Ålander, whose father, both grandfathers, uncles and two brothers had all been shipmasters. Of wiry build, Eriksson had come up through the ranks and was a strict, driving master.

Under her two captains, dissimilar in all but their affection for the lovely bark, the *Herzogin Cecilie* performed handsomely. It was the custom of windjammer skippers to engage in races home from Australia with their cargoes of grain. Usually these so-called grain races were two-ship affairs, as the windjammers left the port facilities in pairs. The idea was not really one of economic gain, since grain was all but imperishable and prices remained more or less stable once they were set for the season. Nevertheless, speed was judged to be the measure of a master's skill and a ship's mettle, and so every captain worth his papers piled on all the canvas he could prudently carry. Old Pjutte Gusta may even have paid a bonus or two for particularly swift passages—although, of course, he would not have wanted word to get out of such wild extravagance.

The *Herzogin Cecilie*'s first trip was her worst: 151 days in 1926 from Port Lincoln, at Spencer Gulf, to Falmouth. Her best was her last: 86 days in 1936 from Port Victoria to Falmouth. Making the homeward trip from the grain ports in fewer than 100 days—"breaking the hundred" it was called—was an aspiration of nearly all Gustaf Erikson's masters. Of the 272 passages between 1921 and 1936 by square-riggers, only 29 broke the hundred. Of these, the *Herzogin Cecilie* led the list, with four.

After her final sparkling 86-day run from Port Victoria in 1936, the *Herzogin Cecilie* put in at Falmouth for orders and then, at 8:20 p.m. on Friday, April 24, set sail for Ipswich to discharge her grain. She stood out on the starboard tack in a moderate sea amid patches of fog, passed well clear of the dangerous Manacle Point, near Lizard Point, and made the last of five course corrections at 3:30 a.m., hauling out 5° in order to give herself more sea room. She was doing seven knots in thick fog. At 3:50 a.m., off the South Devon coast, someone on watch saw—or sensed—a solid mass in the fog on the port side. Captain Sven Eriksson was immediately called, the helm was put hard astarboard and the starboard braces were let run. All too late. The *Herzogin Cecilie* holed herself on Ham Stone Rock, was carried stern first by a swell into Sewer Mill Cove,

The great grain races from down under

Year	Ship	Country
1921	Marlborough Hill	Finland
1922	Milverton	Finland
1923	Beatrice	Sweden
1924	Greif	Germany
1925	Beatrice	Sweden
1926	Avenir	Belgium
1927	Herzogin Cecilie	
1928	Herzogin Cecilie	
1929	Archibald Russell	
1930	Pommern	
1931	Herzogin Cecilie	Finland
1932	Parma	
	Pamir	
1933	Parma	
1934	Passat	
1935	Priwall	Germany
1936	Herzogin Cecilie	
1937	Pommern	
	Passat	Finland
1938	Passat	
1939	Moshulu	

The brain storm in 1928 of a publicity-minded marine paint company, this elaborate globe, six inches in diameter, was the only trophy ever given to a winner of the unofficial but highly competitive grain races from Australia to the British Isles. The Finnish bark Herzogin Cecilie (formerly a German vessel) won it with a passage of 96 days, trouncing her archrival, the Swedish Beatrice, by 18 days. But as can be seen from the chart above, that was nowhere near the overall record.

91 days, Port Lincoln to Queenstown
90 days, Melbourne to London
88 days, Melbourne to London
110 days, Port Lincoln to Falmouth
103 days, Adelaide to Falmouth
110 days, Geelong to Lizard Point
98 days, Port Lincoln to Queenstown
96 days, Port Lincoln to Falmouth
93 days, Melbourne to Queenstown
105 days, Wallaroo to Falmouth
93 days, Wallaroo to Falmouth
103 days, Port Broughton to Falmouth
103 days, Wallaroo to Queenstown
83 days, Port Victoria to Falmouth
106 days, Wallaroo to Lizard Point
91 days, Port Victoria to Queenstown
86 days, Port Lincoln to Falmouth
94 days, Port Victoria to Falmouth
94 days, Port Lincoln to Falmouth
98 days, Port Victoria to Falmouth
91 days, Port Victoria to Queenstown

struck more rock and held fast about 50 yards from the base of a cliff.

Captain Eriksson attributed the wreck of the *Herzogin Cecilie* to a combination of fog, possible magnetic attraction and tides strong enough to throw the ship off course. Then and now the explanation seems frustratingly inadequate. In 1937, only a year after the *Herzogin Cecilie* had foundered, her chronicler, W. L. A. Derby, asked a question that remains pertinent—and unanswered—to this day: "Why should a well-found barque, in capable hands, deviate so far from her intended course that, after logging less than 50 miles, she found herself in dire distress almost ten miles to the north of her calculated position?" Some of the crew later suggested that there was no officer on deck that fateful night until it was too late. There was also the suggestion that, after so splendid a passage, celebrations had been in progress among the crew.

By every reasonable standard, the *Herzogin Cecilie* was already a total loss. But the old windjammer died hard, and her pain was prolonged. Although Britain had been among the first to abandon sail for steam, there now arose in the British public a welling of sympathy and affection for the stricken ship. In mid-May a remarkable appeal for contributions to a salvage and repair fund appeared in British newspapers. The moving force behind the appeal was Captain Sven Eriksson, encouraged by his wife, who loved the ship almost as much as her husband. They had been receiving letters of sympathy after the accident, a number of them enclosing contributions to any fund that might be started to save the famous old windjammer. The Erikssons enlisted the press, which broadcast the plea: "By hundreds of letters and telegrams the British public have made it clear that their interest in sail is genuine and their sympathy for the 'Duchess' profound. Only through sentiment and rigid economy has the owner of *Herzogin Cecilie* been able to maintain his fleet of sailing ships. Should the public help the 'Duchess' to sail the seas again, Captain Sven Eriksson guarantees that the owner, Gustaf Erikson, will take not less than six and up to ten British apprentices yearly, free of all fees, to gain their experience in sail before the mast."

Ludicrous as that offer may have seemed, the public subscription, augmented by a charge of one shilling sixpence for sightseers to come aboard the stranded bark, rose to more than $3,000, an impressive sum in those Depression days. And for his dearest ship, old Gusta was reported ready to make a supreme sacrifice. He was, it was said, willing to spend up to $9,000—almost half of what the *Herzogin Cecilie* had cost him—for repairs if the ship could first be refloated. On June 19 two tugs made the refloating attempt, straining at their cables until the *Herzogin Cecilie* shuddered, moved forward—and finally floated free to sea.

She was towed to nearby Starehole Bay, where more work was to be done on her. By now, noxious gas from the rotting grain in the holds had infiltrated the entire ship, eating away paint and varnish, corroding the hull—and one day overcoming Sven Eriksson, who was found lying in the bilge water. Eriksson recovered, but the *Herzogin Cecilie* could not.

Like many such places on the Devon coast, Starehole Bay was not much more than a shallow cove, open to ground swells and under some conditions to storm waves. One day a swell rolled in from the southeast and forced the windjammer deep into the sand, where she again found

rock beneath her keel. On the night of July 17, a sudden gale finished the job: the seas lifted her, then flung her down again. After 84 days of agony, the *Herzogin Cecilie*'s back was finally broken.

A light and a joy was gone from the life of Gustaf Erikson. But he stuck doggedly to his trade until World War II finally completed what World War I had begun: the twilight era of the windjammers. When Erikson died in 1947, his firm turned quickly to steam. The old man had hoped to pass on a still-going windjammer concern to his youngest son, Gustaf Adolf, who shared his father's love of the great ships. But Gustaf Adolf had died a few years before, and the company went to an older son, who was a businessman pure and simple, with no experience at sea.

By then, in any case, there were only a handful of windjammers afloat and still capable of raising sail. A number of them met their end in the scrap yards of Europe, sliced up by the ship breakers' acetylene torches for their metal; others simply rusted away to jagged hulks in obscure back harbors. A few were preserved as monuments to a bygone age. Erikson's *Passat* became a floating museum at Lübeck, his *Viking* was retired to Gothenburg, Sweden, and his mighty *Pommern* remained as a memorial at Mariehamn itself. Other windjammers—the *Star of India* and the *Balclutha*—were enshrined at San Diego and San Francisco, California. And one, alas, the *Moshulu*, became a restaurant, moored to a wharf at Philadelphia, on the Delaware River.

A very few found a sort of life after death sailing as cadet training vessels, tradition-encrusted symbols of the seafaring past for modern navies. The Laeisz firm's *Padua* became a war reparation from Germany to the Soviet Union and, as the renamed *Kruzenshtern*, could be seen from time to time plying the oceans crowded with aspiring young naval officers. In the 1950s and 1960s a number of nations operated windjammer replicas as showpiece training vessels: among them were the U.S. Coast Guard's *Eagle*, Argentina's *Libertad*, West Germany's *Gorch Fock II* and Denmark's *Danmark*, all setting between 20 and 30 sails and manned by 200 to 300 cadets getting a first whiff of salt.

But for the old windjammers, those deep-laden cargo carriers sailed by a few leathery-faced mariners in the remote reaches of the world's oceans, the era had come to a final close. The last of them in commercial trade that anyone knew about was a four-masted iron bark under Peruvian ownership that ran guano down the Chilean coast. She sank in the Pacific with 3,000 tons of guano on June 26, 1958. Her name: *Omega*, the final letter in the Greek alphabet, signifying the end.

Framed for a moment in the starboard rigging of a passing yacht, the Herzogin Cecilie glides gracefully under full sail across the sun-flecked Baltic Sea in the early 1930s. A profitable globe-tramping cargo carrier even in these late years, she was a rare sight in her own home waters; she returned in ballast like this to Mariehamn only five times in all her 15 years under the flag of the Erikson fleet.

Of rocks and wrecks and "a gathering of murderers"

While fearsome Cape Horn swallowed many a windjammer and crew without trace into the infinite violence of the Southern seas, the ultimate graveyard of the tall ships was 8,000 miles northeast in Britain's granite-fanged Scilly Isles and the headlands of Cornwall. Here steamships, coastal vessels, fishing boats and windjammers by the scores piled up their woeful bones, and the crosstrees of fractured masts gave mute evidence of the final resting place of the proudest and greatest wind-powered machines of all time.

All those ships met their doom so near home ports because of a conspiracy of insidious tides and currents, sepulchral fogs, diabolical gales and monstrous seas that deluded their compasses, betrayed their helms, baffled their pilots and flung their hulls upon the reefs.

One observer compared the rocks to "a great gathering of murderers." Lying 25 miles off Land's End, the 50-odd islets of the Scillies (below) cover only 50 square miles. But in November of 1893 alone, 298 ships were lost there. Together with the gnarled finger of Cornwall, the Scillies divide the Bristol Channel from the English Channel, endangering ships trying to find their way into one channel or the other. Beyond the Scillies in the English Channel lie Lizard Point and Manacle Point, both waiting to trap and disembowel ships groping through night or fiendish storms.

The disasters recorded on the following pages—pictures taken in the final agonies of each ship's life—were photographed by the Gibson family, resident in the Scillies since the 18th Century. Few vessels remained intact for long among the surf-lashed rocks, but while they did they seldom failed to draw scavengers and curiosity seekers. One visitor to the scene, finding in them a tragic beauty, likened the shattered hulks to "vanished masterpieces of great sculptors."

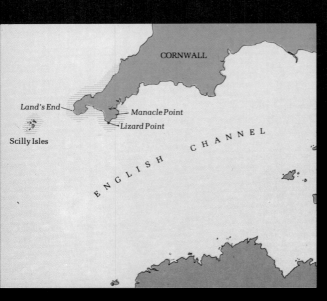

Blown ashore and dismasted in Perran Bay in December 1900, the elegant French

windjammer Seine is explored on a calm day by curious schoolboys and a man riding the broken bowsprit.

Impaled in fog on the Lizard in April 1912, the sleek Gunvor spills Chilean nitrates from ruptured sides. Her Norwegian crew escaped down a rope ladder, at

her bowsprit. Rowboats full of local wreckers later came out to hunt for salvage.

Helpless and abandoned after a week of lying on the rocks of the Lizard, the Cromdale is finally battered to bits by gale-driven seas on May 30, 1913. Inbound fro

Chile with a load of nitrates, the ill-fated vessel ran aground in one of the dense fogs for which the area is famous.

*Smashed on the Lizard in November **1911** en route from Sweden to Australia with timber and pig iron, the square-rigged Hansy dumps her lumber, to the delight*

of local fishermen, who resold it for a pretty price. A salvage party found two goats dozing in a seaman's bunk.

Aground on the Manacles in December 1901, the Glenbervie falls prey to what might be termed a double disaster. To the despair of the wreckers, officials salvaged

her cargo of thousands of cases and barrels of whiskey, leaving only a shipment of waterlogged pianos.

Bibliography

Allen, Jerry, *The Sea Years of Joseph Conrad*. Doubleday, 1965.

Attiwill, Ken, *Windjammer*. Doubleday, 1931.

Barker, James P., *The Log of a Limejuicer*. Huntington Press, 1933.

Binns, Archie, *Northwest Gateway*. Binfords & Mort, 1941.

Bone, David W., *The Brassbounder*. Duckworth, 1910.

Bradford, Gershom, *The Mariner's Dictionary*. Weathervane Books, 1952.

Braynard, Frank O., *Search for the Tall Ships*. Operation Ship, Ltd., 1977.

Carse, Robert, *The Twilight of Sailing Ships*. Galahad Books, 1965.

Clements, Rex:
A Gipsy of the Horn. Heath Cranton, 1924.
A Stately Southerner. Houghton Mifflin, 1926.

Colton, J. F., *Windjammers Significant*. J. F. Colton, 1954.

Coman, Edwin T., Jr., and Helen M. Gibbs, *Time, Tide and Timber*. Greenwood Press, 1968.

Coolidge, Olivia, *The Three Lives of Joseph Conrad*. Houghton Mifflin, 1972.

Cox, Thomas R., *Mills and Markets*. University of Washington Press, 1974.

Dana, R. H., Jr., *The Seaman's Manual*. E. Moxon, 1871.

Derby, W. L. A., *The Tall Ships Pass*. David and Charles, 1937.

Desmond, Shaw, *Windjammer: The Book of the Horn*. Hutchinson, 1932.

Duncan, Fred B., *Deepwater Family*. Pantheon Books, 1969.

Eriksson, Pamela. *The Life and Death of the Duchess*. Houghton Mifflin, 1959.

Fischer, Anton Otto, *Focs'le Days*. Scribner's, 1947.

Fischer, Katrina, *Anton Otto Fischer—Marine Artist*. Teredo Books, 1977.

Fowles, John, *Shipwreck*. Little, Brown, 1974.

Gibbs, Jim:
Pacific Square-Riggers. Bonanza Books, 1969.
West Coast Windjammers in Story and Pictures. Bonanza Books, 1968.

Gowlland, Gladys M. O., *Master of the Moving Sea*. J. F. Colton, 1959.

Hamecher, Horst, *Königin der See Fünfmast-Vollschiff Preussen*. Verlag Egon Heinemann, 1969.

Hennessy, Mark W., *The Sewall Ships of Steel*. The Kennebec Journal Press, 1937.

Henningsen, Henning, *Crossing the Equator*. Munksgaard, 1961.

Hinz, Heinrich, *Under Count Luckner as Seaman First Class*. Ernte-Verlag, 1922.

Hoehling, A. A., *The Great War at Sea: A History of Naval Action 1914-1918*. Thomas Y. Crowell, 1965.

Hoyt, Edwin P., *Count von Luckner: Knight of the Sea*. David McKay, 1969.

Hugill, Stan, *Sailortown*. E. P. Dutton, 1967.

Hurst, Alexander A.:
Arthur Briscoe—Marine Artist, His Life and Work. Teredo Books, 1974.
The Call of High Canvas. Cassell, 1958.
Ghosts on the Sea-Line. Cassell, 1957.
Square-Riggers—The Final Epoch, 1921-1958. Teredo Books, 1972.

Hutton, W. M., *Cape Horn Passage*. Blackie and Son, 1934.

Huycke, Harold D., Jr.:
"The Great Star Fleet." *Yachting*, Feb. 1960.
To Santa Rosalia, Further and Back. Mariner's Museum of Newport News, Va., 1970.

Jean-Aubrey, G., *Joseph Conrad Life and Letters*, Vols. I, II. Heinemann, 1927.

Jobé, Joseph, ed., *The Great Age of Sail*. Crescent Books, 1967.

Johnson, Captain Irving, *The Peking Battles Cape Horn*. Sea History Press, 1977.

Jones, William H. S., *The Cape Horn Breed*. Criterion Books, 1956.

Karlsson, Elis, *Mother Sea*. Oxford University Press, 1964.

Le Scal, Yves, *The Great Days of the Cape Horners*. Souvenir Press, 1966.

Learmont, James S., *Master in Sail*. Percival Marshall, 1950.

Lubbock, Basil:
The Down Easters. Brown, Son & Ferguson, 1929.
The Last of the Windjammers. Brown, Son & Ferguson, 1929.
The Nitrate Clippers. Brown, Son & Ferguson, 1932.

Lucia, Ellis, *The Big Woods*. Doubleday, 1975.

Luckner, Felix von, *Pirate von Luckner and the Cruise of the Seeadler*. Geddis and Blomfield, 1919.

Lydenberg, Harry Miller, *Crossing the Line*. The New York Public Library, 1957.

McCulloch, John Herries, *A Million Miles in Sail*. Dodd, Mead, 1933.

McCutchan, Philip, *Tall Ships: The Golden Age of Sail*. Crown Publishers, 1976.

McEwen, W. A., and A. H. Lewis, *Encyclopedia of Nautical Knowledge*. Cornell Maritime Press, 1953.

MacMullen, Jerry, *Star of India: The Log of an Iron Ship*. Howell-North, 1961.

Masefield, John, *The Wanderer of Liverpool*. Heinemann, 1930.

Masters, David, *The Plimsoll Mark*. Cassell, 1955.

May, W. E., Commander, *A History of Marine Navigation*. Norton, 1973.

Meyer, Jürgen, *Hamburg's Segelschiffe, 1795-1945*. Verlag Egon Heinemann, 1971.

Morgan, Murray, *The Northwest Corner*. Viking, 1962.

Newby, Eric:
Grain Race. George Allen and Unwin, 1968.
The Last Grain Race. Secker & Warburg, 1956.

Noall, Cyril, *Cornish Lights and Shipwrecks*. D. Bradford Barton, 1968.

Peters, George H., *The Plimsoll Line*. Barry Rose, 1975.

Riesenberg, Felix, *Cape Horn*. Dodd, Mead, 1939.

Rohrbach, H. C. Paul, with Captain J. Hermann Piening and Captain A. E. Schmidt, *FL: A Century and a Quarter of Reederei F. Laeisz*. J. F. Colton, 1957.

Spiers, A. G., *The Wavertree: An Ocean Wanderer*. South Street Seaport, 1969.

The Visual Encyclopedia of Nautical Terms under Sail. Crown, 1978.

Thesleff, Holger, *Farewell Windjammer*. Thames and Hudson, 1951.

Thomas, Lowell, *The Sea Devil's Fo'c'sle*. Doubleday, 1929.

Tod, Giles, "Along the Road to Rio." *Yachting*, May 1943.

Tryckare, Tre, ed., *The Lore of Ships*. Crescent Books, 1963.

Underhill, Harold A., *Deep-Water Sail*. Brown, Son & Ferguson, 1976.

Villiers, J. Alan:
By Way of Cape Horn. Scribner's, 1952.
Falmouth for Orders. Scribner's, 1952.
Last of the Wind Ships. George Routledge, 1934.
Men, Ships and the Sea. National Geographic Society, 1973.
Sea-Dogs of To-day. George G. Harrap, 1932.
Voyage of the Parma. Geoffrey Bles, 1933.
The War with Cape Horn. Scribner's, 1971.
The Way of a Ship. Scribner's, 1970.

Villiers, Alan, and Henri Picard, *The Bounty Ships of France*. Scribner's, 1972.

Woolard, Claude L. A., ed., *The Last of the Cape Horners*. Arthur H. Stockwell, 1967.

Picture Credits

Cover: Eileen Tweedy, painting by Derek G. M. Gardner, R.S.M.A., courtesy National Maritime Museum, London. Front and back end papers: Drawing by Peter McGinn. Page 3: Al Freni, courtesy The National Maritime Historical Society, Brooklyn, N.Y. 6, 7: Alan Villiers from Popperfoto, London. 8, 9: National Maritime Museum at San Francisco, Halvorson Collection. 10, 11: National Maritime Museum at San Francisco, Page Collection. 12, 13: Alan Villiers from Popperfoto, London. 14, 15: Jean Randier Collection, Paris. 16, 17: Courtesy Kennedy Galleries, New York. 19: Foto Pozzar, courtesy Museo Civico di Belle Arti, Trieste. 20: Courtesy Mystic Seaport, Inc., Mystic, Conn. 23: Fischer-Daber, courtesy Altonaer Museum, Hamburg. 26: National Maritime Museum at San Francisco. 29: Courtesy The Mariner's Museum of Newport News, Va. 30, 31, 32: Drawings by John Batchelor. 34, 35: Drawings by Peter McGinn. 36: National Maritime Museum, London. 38: National Maritime Museum at San Francisco, Hester Collection. 42: Private Collection, Paris. 44, 45: National Maritime Museum at San Francisco, Hester Collection, except top left, National Maritime Museum at San Francisco. 47: National Maritime Museum at San Francisco. 49:

The Beinecke Rare Book and Manuscript Library, Yale University. 52, 53: Jean Randier Collection, Paris. 55: National Maritime Museum at San Francisco. 57: Alan Villiers from Popperfoto, London. 58: Courtesy Captain J. Ferrell Colton. 60 through 63: Reproduced from *Anton Otto Fischer —Marine Artist* by permission of Teredo Books Ltd., Brighton. 64: Frank Lerner, courtesy Katrina Sigsbee Fischer. 65, 66, 67: Reproduced from *Anton Otto Fischer —Marine Artist* by permission of Teredo Books Ltd., Brighton. 68, 69: Courtesy Dr. Jürgen Meyer, Rellingen, Germany. 72: Fischer-Daber, courtesy F.·Laeisz, Hamburg. 73: Fischer-Daber, courtesy Museum für Hamburgische Geschichte, Hamburg. 75: Courtesy Norman Brouwer. 77 through 80: Drawings by John Batchelor. 82: Dmitri Kessel, courtesy Musée International du Long-Cours Cap Horniers, Saint Malo. 83: Sammlung Bernartz im Deutsches Schiffahrtsmuseum, Bremerhaven. 84, 85: H. Roger-Viollet, Paris. 87: National Maritime Museum at San Francisco—Courtesy Bath Marine Museum, Bath, Me. 88, 89: Peabody Museum of Salem. 92: National Maritime Museum at San Francisco. 93: National Maritime Museum at San Francisco, Hester Collection. 94: Library of Congress. 96 through 101: Reproduced from *Arthur Briscoe—Marine Artist, His Life and Work* by permission of Teredo Books Ltd., Brighton. 102, 103: Jiri Juru, courtesy Goemans Col-

lection, Schoten, Belgium. 106: Map by William Hezlep. 108, 109: National Maritime Museum at San Francisco, Plummer Collection. 110: Alan Villiers. 112, 113: Alan Villiers from Popperfoto, London. 116: The South Street Seaport Museum, New York. 120: Deutsches Schiffahrtsmuseum, Bremerhaven. 122: Erwin Böhm, Mainz, courtesy Heinrich Graf Luckner, Oberursel. 125: Reproduced from *The Sea Devil, The Story of Count Felix von Luckner, The German War Raider* by Lowell Thomas, William Heinemann Ltd., London, 1928. 127 through 132: Paulus Leeser, courtesy Peter Kircheisz Collection, Ontario. 133: Map by William Hezlep. 134: Paulus Leeser, courtesy Peter Kircheisz Collection, Ontario. 136 through 143: Drawings by Richard Schlecht. 144, 145: Cookson Collection, Long Sutton, Lincolnshire, England. 146, 147: Folkes Foto, courtesy Ålands Sjöfartsmuseum, Mariehamn, Finland. 149: National Maritime Museum at San Francisco—Peabody Museum of Salem. 150, 152: Alan Villiers from Popperfoto, London. 154, 155: Reproduced from *Last of the Wind Ships* by Alan J. Villiers, George Routledge Sons Ltd., London, 1934. 157: Folkes Foto, courtesy Ålands Sjöfartsmuseum, Mariehamn, Finland. 158, 159: Courtesy Dr. Jürgen Meyer, Rellingen, Germany. 160, 161: Map by William Hezlep; F. E. Gibson, Scilly Isles. 162 through 169: F. E. Gibson, Scilly Isles.

Acknowledgments

The index for this book was prepared by Gale Partoyan. The editors wish to thank John Batchelor, artist *(pages 30-32, 77-80)*, Peter McGinn, artist *(end-paper maps)*, Richard Schlecht, artist, and William Avery Baker, consultant *(pages 136-143)*.

The editors also wish to thank: In Australia: Ross Osmond, Adelaide. In Belgium: Annick Goemans, Schoten. In Canada: Peter Kircheisz, Toronto. In Finland: Lars Grönstrand, Abo; Christian Ulfstedt, Helsinki; Captain Karl Kåhre, Curator, Ålands Sjöfartsmuseum, Mariehamn. In Germany: Captain Rolf Reinemuth, Bremen-Lesum; Arnold Kludas, Director of Archive and Library, Deutsches Schiffahrtsmuseum, Bremerhaven; Gerhard Kaufmann, Director, Altonaer Museum, Harro Christiansen, Blohm und Voss, Walter Kresse, Museum für Hamburgische Geschichte, Sophie Christine von Mitzlaff-Laeisz, Dieter Jaufmann, Reederei Laeisz, Hamburg; Heinrich Graf Luckner, Oberursel; Captain Walther von Zatorski, Osterholz-Scharmbeck; Heinz Burmester, Wedel-Holstein; Walter Lüden, Friesenmuseum, Wyk auf Föhr. In London: Juliet Carter, P. R. Ince, David Lyon, Ursula Stuart Mason, Joan Moore, Pieter van der Merwe, G. S. Osbon, A. W. H. Pearsall, Roger Quarm, Denis Stonham, David Taylor, National Maritime Museum; David R. MacGregor, Peter M. Wood. Elsewhere in England: Alexander A. Hurst, Brighton; Mark Myers, Bude, Cornwall; Richard M. Cookson, Long Sutton, Lincolnshire. In Paris: Monique de la Roncière, Curator, Bibliothèque Nationale; Gérard Bordes; Robert de Chateaubriand; Irène Delaroière; Gérard Baschet, Editions de *l'Illustration*; Madeleine Farnarier; Fabienne de Fonscolombe; Marie-Thérèse Hirschkoff; Hervé Cras, Director for Documentary Studies, Denise Chaussegroux, Researcher, Musée de la Marine; Hélène Petit; Maryvonne Stéphan. Elsewhere in France: Pierre Lacroix, La Bernerie en Retz; Simone Lambert, Deputy Curator, Musée de la Marine, Chambre de Commerce et d'Industrie, Marseille; Commandant Georges Aubin, Nantes; Commandant Léon Gautier, Raymond Lemaire, Saint Lunaire; Commandant Joseph Hourrière, Dan Lailler, Curator, Musée International du Long-Cours Cap Hornier, Saint Malo; Victor Richard, Saint Servan. In Rome: Marc' Antonio Bragadin; Commander Tullio Serafini, Ministero della Marina. Elsewhere in Italy: Luisa Secchi, Director, Museo Navale, Genoa-Pegli; Giulio Montenero, Director, Museo Civico di Belle Arti, Trieste; Baron Giambattista Rubin de Cervin, Director, Museo Navale, Venice. In Santiago: Julieta Kirkwood, Research Professor, Latin American Faculty of Social Sciences; Leopoldo Benavides, Research Professor, Latin American School of Sociology; Humberto Valenzuela, Director, Museum of Popular and Folkloric Art, Eugenio Pereira Salas, Director, Department of History, University of Chile. In Stockholm: Captain Bengt Ohrelius, Chief of Information, Gösta Webe, Curator, National Maritime Museum. In Tahiti: J. Ferrell Colton.

The editors also wish to thank: In Washington, D.C.: Francis D. Roche, Museum Technician, Richard Philbrick, Division of Transportation, John H. White, Jr., Curator, Division of Transportation, The National Museum of History and Technology, Smithsonian Institution; Charles Haberlein, Agnes Hoover, Naval Historical Center. Elsewhere in the United States: Murray Morgan, Auburn, Wash.; Marnee Lilly, Bath Marine Museum, Bath, Me.; Richard Kaffenberger, Cambridge, Mass.; Captain Irving Johnson, Hadley, Mass.; Philip L. Budlong, Registrar, Mystic Seaport, Inc., Mystic, Conn.; Larry Duane Gilmore, Assistant Curator, Department of Collections, Carolyn Ritger, Photographic Librarian, The Mariners Museum of Newport News, Va.; Norman Brouwer, Historian, The South Street Seaport Museum, Rex Vivian, New York; Ken Dillon, Rosslyn, Va.; Waverly Lowell, John Maounis, National Maritime Museum at San Francisco; Kathy Flynn, Photographic Assistant, Markham W. Sexton, Staff Photographer, Philip C. F. Smith, Curator of Maritime History, Peabody Museum, Salem, Mass.; Harold Sewall Williams, Waitsfield, Vt.

Quotations from *The War with Cape Horn* by Alan Villiers, © 1971 Alan Villiers, and *The Way of a Ship* by Alan Villiers, copyright 1953 by Alan Villiers, are used with permission of Charles Scribner's Sons. Excerpts from *The Sea Devil's Fo'c'sle* by Lowell Thomas and Count Felix von Luckner, copyright 1929 by Lowell Thomas. Reprinted by permission of Doubleday and Company, Inc. Quotations from *The Tall Ships Pass* by W. L. A. Derby reprinted by kind permission of David and Charles, England. Quotations from *A Million Miles in Sail* by John Herries McCulloch, 1933, reprinted by permission of Dodd, Mead and Co. Other particularly valuable sources for this book were: *Focs'le Days* by Anton Otto Fischer, © 1976 Katrina Fischer, Charles Scribner's Sons, 1947; *A Stately Southerner* by Rex Clements, Houghton Mifflin Co., 1926, and *FL: A Century and a Quarter of Reederei F. Laeisz* by H. C. Paul Rohrbach with Captain J. Hermann Piening and Captain A. E. Schmidt, translated by Antoinette G. Smith, J. F. Colton and Co., 1957.

Index

Printed and bound by Artes Gráficas Toledo, S.A., Spain.   D.L.TO:935-1988